# DESIGN
# DRAWING TECHNIQUES
## FOR ARCHITECTS, GRAPHIC DESIGNERS & ARTISTS

## TOM PORTER AND SUE GOODMAN

# Acknowledgments

The authors would like to thank the following people for their help in providing material and information for the production of this book:

Andrew Bradford, Gary Collins, George Dombek, Jack Forman, David Grindley, Ron Hess, Deb Macy, Gordon Kirtley, Mike Leech, Conor O'Sullivan, Ronald Shaeffer, Peter D. Stone, Catherine Tranmer, and Ray Williamson.

Special thanks are due to Pat McNiff for typing the text.

Butterworth Architecture
An imprint of Butterworth-Heinemann Ltd
Linacre House, Jordan Hill, Oxford OX2 8DP

 A member of the Reed Elsevier group

OXFORD  LONDON  BOSTON
MUNICH  NEW DELHI  SINGAPORE  SYDNEY
TOKYO  TORONTO  WELLINGTON

First published by Macmillan Publishing Company 1991
First published in Great Britain 1992
Reprinted 1994

© Tom Porter and Sue Goodman 1991

**British Library Cataloguing in Publication Data**
A catalogue record for this book is available from the British Library

**Library of Congress Cataloguing in Publication Data**
A catalogue record for this book is available from the Library of Congress

ISBN 0 7506 0812 9

Printed and bound in Great Britain by Thomson Litho Ltd, East Kilbride, Scotland

# TABLE OF CONTENTS

# Preface

Design Drawing Techniques has been devised as a graphic resource for the beginning student and as a companion to the four-volume set of Manual of Graphic Techniques. It is intended to help bring a degree of conviction and realism to architectural presentation drawings and has been produced with the knowledge that students, when portraying their building designs with little presentation time, will often resort to drawing entourage from memory rather than make objective studies. More often than not, this approach results in sterile drawings filled with pictorial stylism.

As our memory as to the appearance of everyday objects can be unreliable, the resulting pictorial stylism will often describe a strange, drawing-board world in which an architectural form is hatched against line and dot backgrounds. A world in which bleakness is occasionally punctuated by stereotyped cars and trees or, more rarely, by odd, balloon-shaped people in an attempt to bring life and scale to the starkness of their settings. In adopting this hackneyed form of expression, the student risks relegating the depiction of the building design--and the objects that surround or occupy it--to a common and debased stereotype. At worst, this approach can become as universal in its conformity and professional use as is the potential blandness and anonymity of the architecture it undoubtedly influences. It is no coincidence that successful and well-published architects have each developed their own personalized drawing skills, and Design Drawing Techniques is filled with details taken from their work--each meticulously redrawn by Sue Goodman. In exploring the opportunities for elaboration and detail provided by orthographic and perspective drawings, it is hoped that these examples will form the basis of an understanding of how graphic techniques can best be employed to communicate the various elements of a drawing. Indeed, it is from such an understanding that a convincing and professional-looking graphic can be constructed.

# Introduction: Drawing Types

Representational drawing types in design seem to supply two types of information: either they describe how a space might function, i.e., its organizational aspects; or they describe visual characteristics as perceived by an observer. The range of drawing modes used in design is represented by five basic graphic types that, in providing a variety of viewpoints, allow the designer to make a conceptual journey around the space created by his or her idea. For example, the floor plan positions the mind's eye in the space directly above the linear footprint of the design for an aerial view of its sliced horizontal organization (a). Slicing vertically through the design, the resulting section brings us down to earth for a hovering frontal view of its internal cells, as exposed by a selective cross-cut (b). This horizontal viewpoint is retained by the elevation that affords us a central head-on scrutiny of the massing and silhouette of the outer face of the form (c). However, like the section, the elevation can provide a series of vantage points around the design concept. Whether sliced in sections or an unsliced elevation, the sequential views always depict the elements of the design at the same scale. By offering a three-quarter view of a design, the axonometric introduces the third dimension. This type of drawing, known as a paraline projection, flies us into the ortho-graphic space above the form for a 45-degree-angled reconnaissance of three of its sides (d). A variation of this drawing type is the isometric. It lowers our eye to a viewing angle of 30-degrees, but, like its axono-metric counterpart, the angle can be inverted for a subterranean viewpoint that looks upward and into the interior spaces of a design. By releasing our eye from the fixed viewpoints associated with orthographic drawings, the fifth graphic type extends an ability to make more adventurous excursions into three dimensions. This freedom of vantage point is made possible by the per-spective drawing (e). Coordinated by vanish-ing points, it recognizes the diminishing size of objects with distance, thereby allowing design concepts to be simulated realistically from any preselected viewpoint. Perspective drawings can enlist one, two, or three vanishing points--the greater their number, the greater the distortion of converging planes in the chosen view.

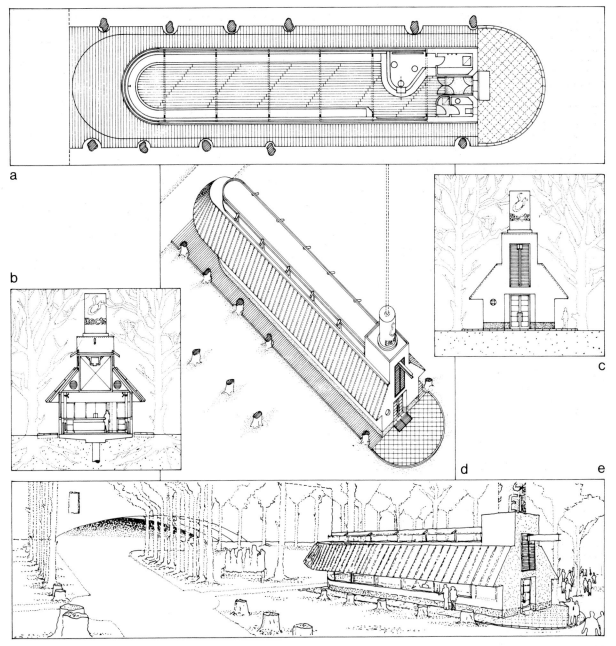

a

b

c

d

e

# Orthographic Scale

When preparing architectural designs, the orthographics (plans, sections, elevations, and paralines) are always drawn to scale, i.e., with their dimensions a particular fractional part of their full size. The drafting instrument that aids this conversion is called a "scale." This is a special ruler that carries, in addition to a scale of feet and inches, markings that represent feet and inches reduced in proportion to one of the usual scales used in architectural drawing. For example, to draft a building design to a scale where, say, 1/4" equals one foot, the calibrations marked 1/4"--found at the end of the ruler--are used. Along this scale, quarter-inch spaces are indicated by 0, 2, 4, 6, and so on. These represent the quarter-inch scale equivalent of feet. The space in front of the zero is subdivided into twelve parts to represent inches in the same scale. At the opposite end of the scale are found similar calibrations for the scale 1/8" equals one foot. Some versions of the scale ruler carry up to twelve different scales.

While the Imperial system of measure is still used in the U.S., most other countries in the world are now on the metric system, which divides a unit of measure into ten rather than twelve parts. On metric scales, a particular metric unit, such as a centimeter, is used to represent a meter.

Selecting a scale for an orthographic drawing is simply a means of regulating what the designer sees in his head and the size or degree of complexity of the presented design. For instance, plans, sections, and elevations are usually drafted at 1/4" = 1'-0" or 1/8" = 1'-0" (metric equivalents 1:50 or 1:100), but a scale of 1/2" = 1'-0" (1:20) allows details to be focused. Increasingly smaller scales, which increase the distance between the viewer and the size of the building, are used for larger edifices and building complexes. These are shrunk along a decreasing scale of 1/16" = 1'-0" (1:200) or 1:500. Thus, in selecting a scale, the designer not only regulates the distance of an idea from his mind's eye, he also regulates its graphic size so that it will fit within the confines of the drawing format. Then, too, as the scale of a drawing increases, more detail in orthographics and perspectives becomes visible and, with it, the opportunity for introducing a more convincing rendition of the objects and forms that will have impact on the architectural design.

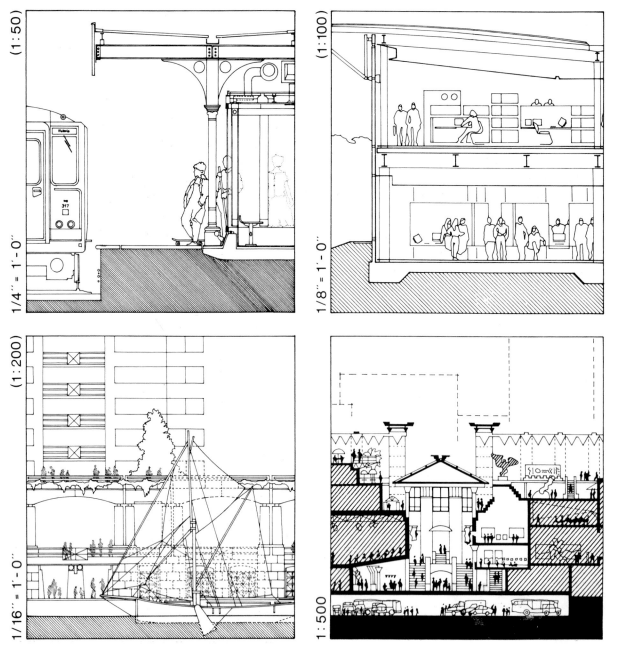

# Line Quality and Drawing Style

Drawing is very much like handwriting. Indeed, being instantly recognizable, the personalized drawing styles of many architects act rather like "signatures," such as in the way we can quickly spot a "Paul Rudolph," a "Frank Lloyd Wright," or a "Michael Graves."

At the heart of every drawing style, however, is the development of line quality, and as in handwriting, there are many variations. In Design Drawing Techniques, however, we have, in the main, concentrated on ink-line examples, but it should be mentioned that the technical pen is not exclusive to design drawings, and that the chosen medium has a strong effect on the quality of line.

Line quality can vary from the scratchy (a) and the sinuous (b), to the aggressively bold and simple. Lines can also exist in the nervous frequency of a broken line (c), or in the deliberate accuracy of a continuous hardline (d). Furthermore, a rich variety of line quality can be found within the design sequences of individual designers--the use of different drawing attitudes for different points along the design process. But these individual qualities of line and styles of drawing did not evolve from any conscious effort on the part of their delineators. Rather, they mirror the personality of the designer and exist as a by-product of the design philosophy that generated them together with the intention of the drawing. Indeed, a common denominator between these drawings is that their linear techniques act in a subservient role to the information being communicated.

Therefore, in seeking a graphic vocabulary that will enhance the degree of realism so important to the representation of abstract architectural ideas, the reader should recognize that a truly personal drawing ability grows primarily from within. It begins, of course, by using our eyes, by sketching what we see, and by experimenting with line-making mediums and their potential for making other kinds of marks.

# Rendering

The introduction of value to a line drawing is a natural step. It responds to a need to increase a sense of solidity and depth to the spatial illusion through the effect of light, shade, and shadow. Traditionally, architectural drawings were rendered with washes of Chinese ink, but these days, the vast majority of design drawings--aside from those rendered with the tones of dry-transfer screens--are shaded with graphite or colored pencils, or hatched with pen and ink.

Therefore, alongside a familiarity with different types of line, the beginning student should also master a vocabulary of tone. This can be achieved through sketchbook experience, experiment, and exercise, but another strategy is to study the details of drawings made by master draftsmen, such as Franco Purini, whose work appears elsewhere in this book. Purini's drawings are a good example because they function almost as graphic essays of value-rendering techniques. Indeed, to isolate just a few of his linear-based textural treatments and tones compiles a veritable dictionary of highly controlled marks that simulate a rich range of surface effects.

Beyond the mastering of value-rendering techniques, we must also learn how to organize them in a drawing. For instance, it would be pointless to treat the eye to a rich array of technical skill while the main point of the drawing, i.e., the building design, was smothered. Therefore, the extension of line into value is not only a means of emphasizing architectural space, it is also a process of structuring the rendered and unrendered areas to create a framework for steering the eye around the drawing format. Not only can a selective and sparse use of tone for indicating surface and shadow in a site plan highlight, at a minimal level, the nature of visible planes and the unseen vertical mass, but it can also target the building in its setting. Conversely, when an intensive and exhaustive rendering is employed across the drawing format, it is the white and unrendered areas that become the center of attention. Therefore, the decision to render a drawing is an activity involving the graphic organization of positive (black) and negative (white) elements. Furthermore, successful drawings result when concentrations of highest contrast in the tonal structure coincide with the most important message areas of the drawing.

# Visual Interest

A further aspect of design drawing that should be considered in the preliminary stages of a drawing is visual interest. One aspect of visual interest is the fascination caused by a contrast between different types of mark, such as the difference between the ruled outline of a building and the freehand movement of a line describing foliage (a). Graphic interest is also illustrated by the juxtaposition of highly disciplined marks and those made apparently by accident or in the heat of the moment. This juxtaposition of the graphically "deliberate" and "dashing" can be found in the work of many architects who exploit this form of contrast to various degrees. It is, however, a strategy that lies at the heart of the success of many architectural drawings (b).

The considered arrangement of marks and the forms and spaces they describe on paper is called "composition"--and it controls another aspect of visual interest. For example, evenly balanced compositions can appear predictable and boring. Much more interesting visually is the counterbalancing of forms and textures of dissimilar size and unequal weight (c). The visual tension set up between components of counterbalanced and asymmetrical compositions are more provoking and, therefore, of more interest to the eye (d). Also, when composing graphics and, especially, perspectives, care should be taken to allow the eye to wander about the spaces created by the drawing. This approach to composition responds to the idea of entertaining the spectator and encouraging his or her eye to engage in the drawing and explore its format while absorbing information. It is also diametrically opposed to the idea of placing elements, such as trees or figures, at the dead center of a perspective, of positioning them like bookends to either side of an elevation, or allowing the heads and shoulders of foreground figures to pop-up from the lower portion of the format and block the space implied by the drawing. This pattern of visual interest is referred to by the author William Kirby Lockard. He uses the analogy of a bouncing ball to demonstrate the movement of the viewer's eye into and about the depth of space in a drawing.

a

b

c

d

# Functions of Entourage

For the purposes of this book, entourage includes all the props, accessories, and embellishments that are likely to bring a dimension of reality and an increased sense of scale and animation to orthographic diagrams and perspectives. The vast majority of those illustrated in this book are from the work of practicing architects and design students and, among others, include figures, trees, vehicles, furniture, shadows, lettering, etc.

However, the use of architectural entourage should be approached as a means of giving a design drawing a sense of place, i.e., of extending a diagrammatic building proposal into a suggestion of the hypothetical realism of its intended setting. This process begins the moment a tree is added to a site plan or a backdrop to an elevation (a), or when a figure is located in a perspective (b). Even at this minimal level (and design drawing entourage works best when not overstated), this process not only humanizes the design statement but is also a means of testing architectural ideas and measuring them against the objects they would encounter in their intended environments. In this sense, the introduction of contextual information continues rather than terminates the critical process of design. Furthermore, in providing a greater visual understanding of the impact of a proposal to others, this process also widens the critical debate.

Finally, the addition of graphic props to a drawing should not be seen as a means for improving poor designs. Indeed, the introduction of entourage can have quite the opposite effect. For instance, the addition of shadow rendering to an elevation drawing will not improve its design but, instead, may function to expose an inherent weakness in its three-dimensional massing. Therefore, architectural entourage is a design tool that, when used with sensitivity and candor, will immerse an architectural concept in the simulated reality of its context as it brings a new level of meaning to its design.

a

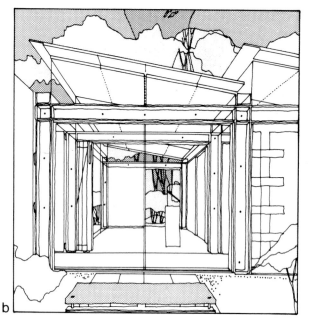

b

# 1 CODES, CUTS, AND CONVENTIONS

# The Convention of Line

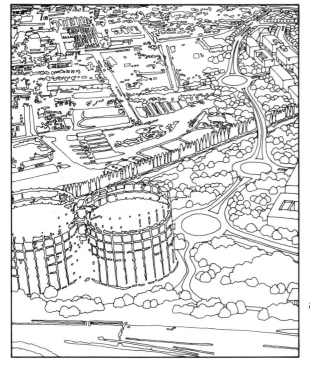

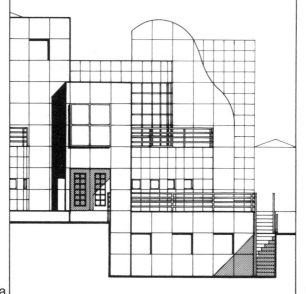

a

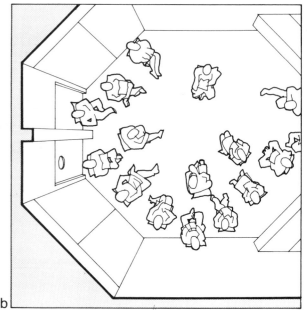

b

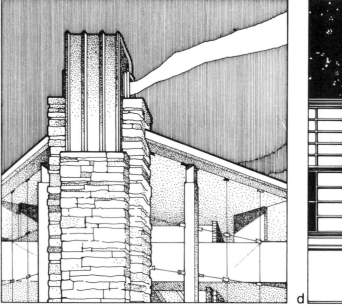

c

d

Line is itself the convention of drawing. Lines in drawings simply describe the edge of forms and shapes seen in our visual perception. We learn from childhood to read these as the contours of objects in graphic form. However, thickness, or weight of line in architectural graphics, can signal different meanings. A basic use of line weight differentiates important from subservient elements, or "near" from "far" (a). A variation on the convention of a diminishing line thickness with distance is also used by some delineators. This refers to a system of line thickness in which thicker lines are reserved for those outlines behind which lies the greatest distance in the drawing (b). Within this system, a skyline contour would be the thickest line because this edge represents the distance between the skyline and infinity (c). Also, the considered deployment of slightly thicker lines on shadow-casting edges of forms and planes in paralines and elevations is a convention that conveys a subtle sense of light and shade (d).

12

# The Convention of Line

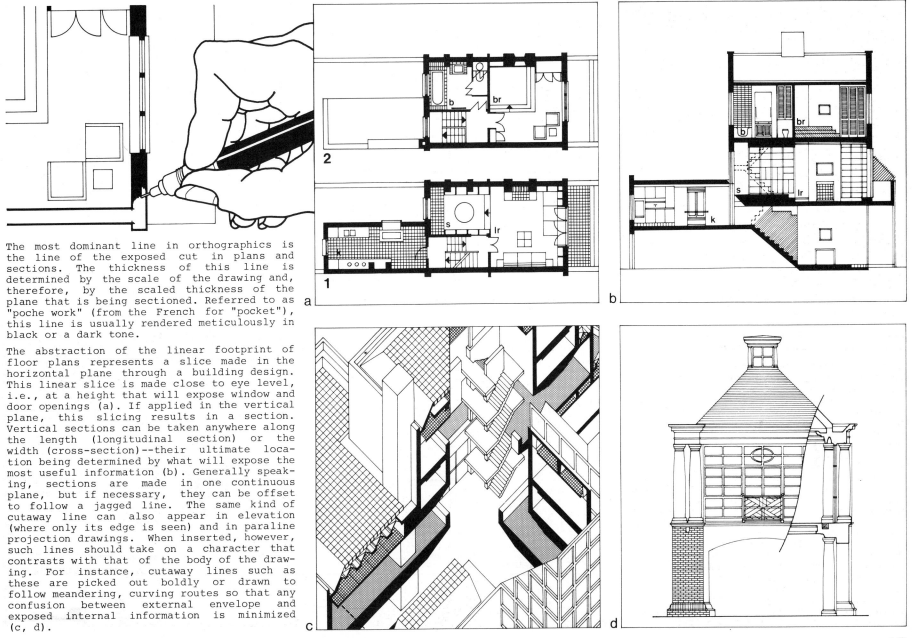

The most dominant line in orthographics is the line of the exposed cut in plans and sections. The thickness of this line is determined by the scale of the drawing and, therefore, by the scaled thickness of the plane that is being sectioned. Referred to as "poche work" (from the French for "pocket"), this line is usually rendered meticulously in black or a dark tone.

The abstraction of the linear footprint of floor plans represents a slice made in the horizontal plane through a building design. This linear slice is made close to eye level, i.e., at a height that will expose window and door openings (a). If applied in the vertical plane, this slicing results in a section. Vertical sections can be taken anywhere along the length (longitudinal section) or the width (cross-section)--their ultimate location being determined by what will expose the most useful information (b). Generally speaking, sections are made in one continuous plane, but if necessary, they can be offset to follow a jagged line. The same kind of cutaway line can also appear in elevation (where only its edge is seen) and in paraline projection drawings. When inserted, however, such lines should take on a character that contrasts with that of the body of the drawing. For instance, cutaway lines such as these are picked out boldly or drawn to follow meandering, curving routes so that any confusion between external envelope and exposed internal information is minimized (c, d).

# The Convention of Line

a

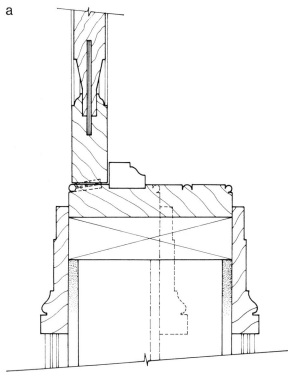

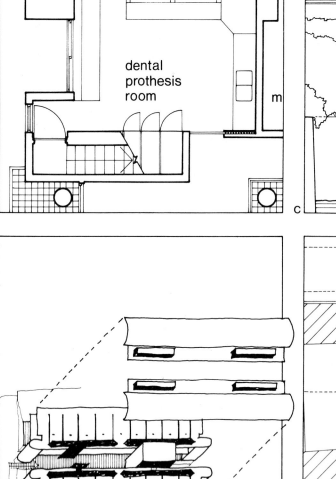

b

dental
prothesis
room

stora

m

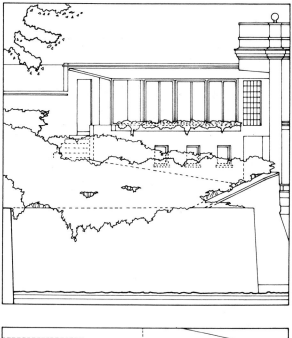

c

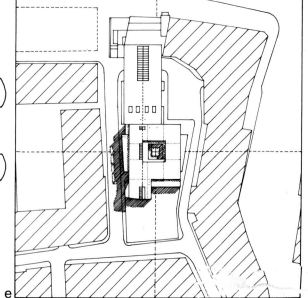

e

Various line conventions are used in ortho-graphics, and each carries a specific mean-ing. The distinctive pulse of a break line is employed to signal the severance of exces-sively long or repetitive elements from a drawing (a). Break lines often denote the removal of a central portion of an element so that its extremities can appear within the drawing format. Break lines are also used to sever staircases as they ascend through the plane described in plans (b). A broken line expressed in dots or short dashes is used to ghost the outlines of relevant forms or planes that are hidden behind or under planes or forms seen in the line of view (c). Broken lines are also enlisted as "stretch lines" in exploded drawings when the direct connection between the fragmented parts of the graphic is ghosted (d). Yet another version of the broken line indicates invis-ible force lines, such as the underlying proportional geometry in elevations, or the trajectory of axial lines in plans (e).

# The Convention of Line

a

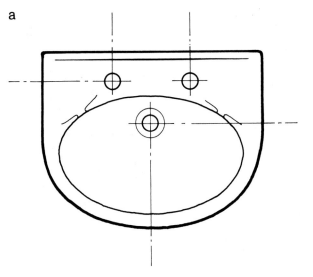

Center lines are a common version of the axial force line. These are more commonly found in elevations and sections and are composed of fine broken lines interspersed with a dot (a). Projection lines appear as a series of extended fine-line dashes. These serve to transfer points from within a drawing to its outer edge (b). Dimension lines are continuous delineations that often work in conjunction with projection lines. These are drafted at the weight of construction lines--their ends being slashed with a short diagonal at the critical points where they precisely cut the projection lines to which they relate (c). Boundary lines are drawn in a bold line and comprise an emphatic system of dashes and dots to diagram the edges of sites in plans or the periphery of zones within a drawing (d). Section lines are important indicators. They are normally drawn boldly on the plan to show the location where a vertical slice has been taken by an accompanying sectional view. In other words, they function as a three-dimensional cross-reference between section and plan. The arrows at each end of the section line should point in the direction of the view and can be accompanied by a letter key that is read in the same direction. This notation allows the attendant section drawing to be titled "Section A-A" or "Section B-B" for identification (e).

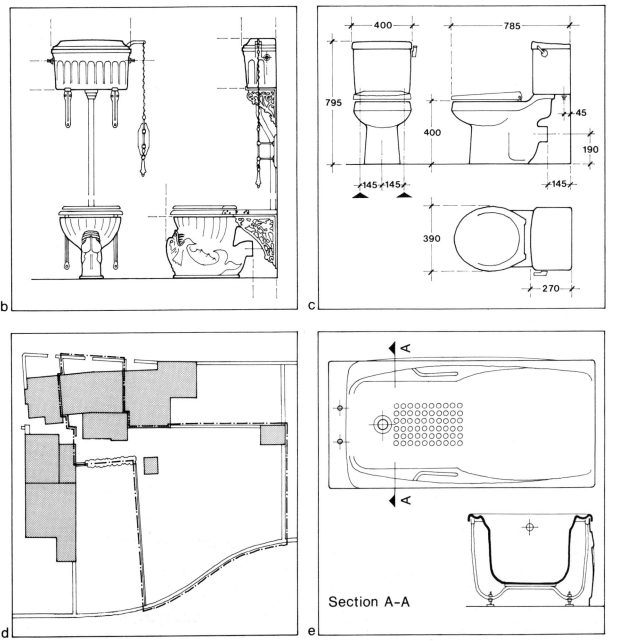

b

c

d

e

Section A-A

# Sectional Cuts

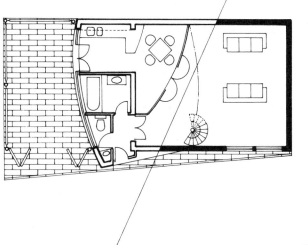

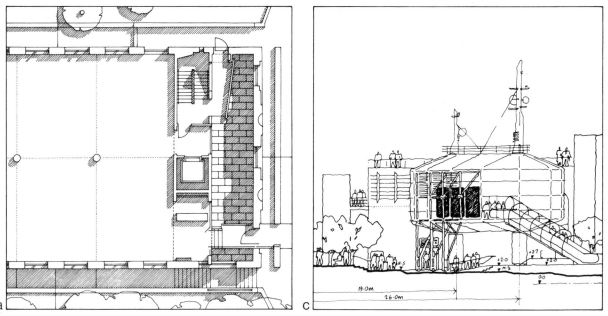

a

c

Whether or not the revealed floor planes of building plans are delineated with furniture and finishes, the abstraction of their sectional slice should remain dominant. In exclusively line-drawn plans, the slice can be emphasized with two slightly heavier outlines or filled in with solid black. When the plan is rendered with shadows, etc., this dominance is achieved by a contrast that is the result of leaving the slice unrendered and white (a). Similarly, when building plans and site sections are exclusively delineated, the profile of the cut can be emphasized together with the profile of the ground line. However, when a building section cut is rendered, the chosen technique can be extended below the ground line, because the vertical slice is seen to continue its cutting action down into the landmass. The graphic recognition of this deeper cut provides the dual function of highlighting the topography and providing a background for titles, etc. (b). The profile of the ground line in elevations can also be represented as a boldly delineated profile or as a deep vertical cut (see facing page). Either way, a space between viewer and facade can be inferred and, if required, animated with entourage, such as figures or trees (c).

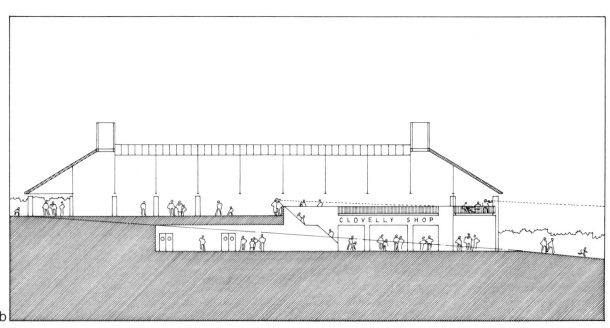

b

# Sectional Cuts in Elevations

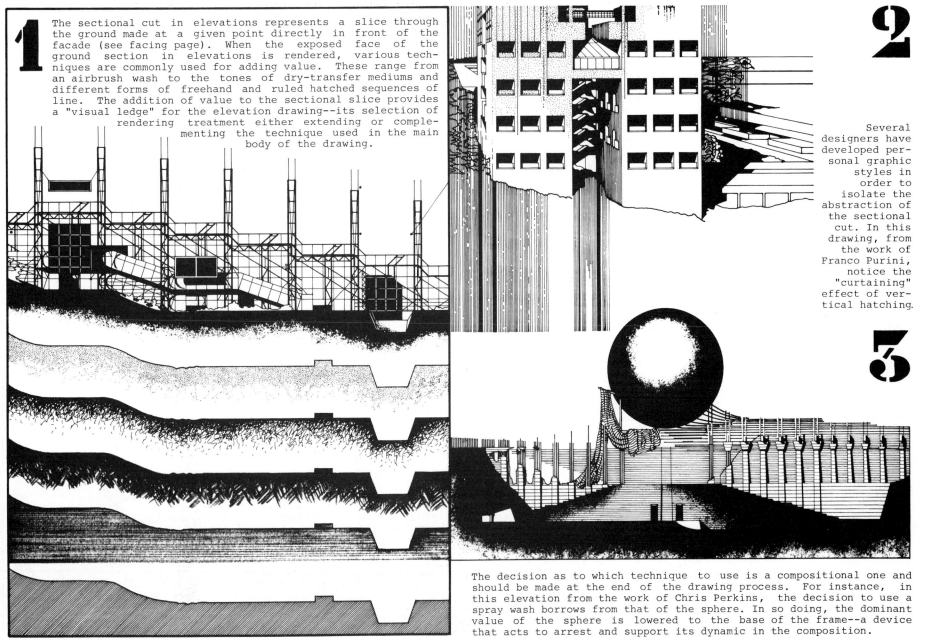

**1** The sectional cut in elevations represents a slice through the ground made at a given point directly in front of the facade (see facing page). When the exposed face of the ground section in elevations is rendered, various techniques are commonly used for adding value. These range from an airbrush wash to the tones of dry-transfer mediums and different forms of freehand and ruled hatched sequences of line. The addition of value to the sectional slice provides a "visual ledge" for the elevation drawing--its selection of rendering treatment either extending or complementing the technique used in the main body of the drawing.

**2** Several designers have developed personal graphic styles in order to isolate the abstraction of the sectional cut. In this drawing, from the work of Franco Purini, notice the "curtaining" effect of vertical hatching.

**3** The decision as to which technique to use is a compositional one and should be made at the end of the drawing process. For instance, in this elevation from the work of Chris Perkins, the decision to use a spray wash borrows from that of the sphere. In so doing, the dominant value of the sphere is lowered to the base of the frame--a device that acts to arrest and support its dynamic in the composition.

# Complex Cuts and Complex Views

This axonometric by Sunand Prasad of an Indian courtyard house makes an L-shaped cut in order to provide visual access to the various levels of the interior, but especially to realize the inner communal courtyard in relation to the other areas of the house. To complete the exposure of this view, notice that the adjacent house has also been cut away using an extension of the horizontal slice. To add clarity to the drawing, a slightly bolder line has been used to outline the sliced portion of the structure, while a minimal stippling is confined to horizontal and vertical planes of the main facade and courtyard.

Aside from physically slicing into an axonometric, another method of "cutting" into the complexities of a building concept is to allow its vertical and horizontal planes to dissolve so as to reveal formal information at the heart of the design. This detail from a bird's-eye axonometric view of a town house design by Peter C. Pran adopts the transparency afforded by the convention of broken lines, which allows lines hidden behind layered planes to become visually accessible (see page 14).

# Animated Drawings

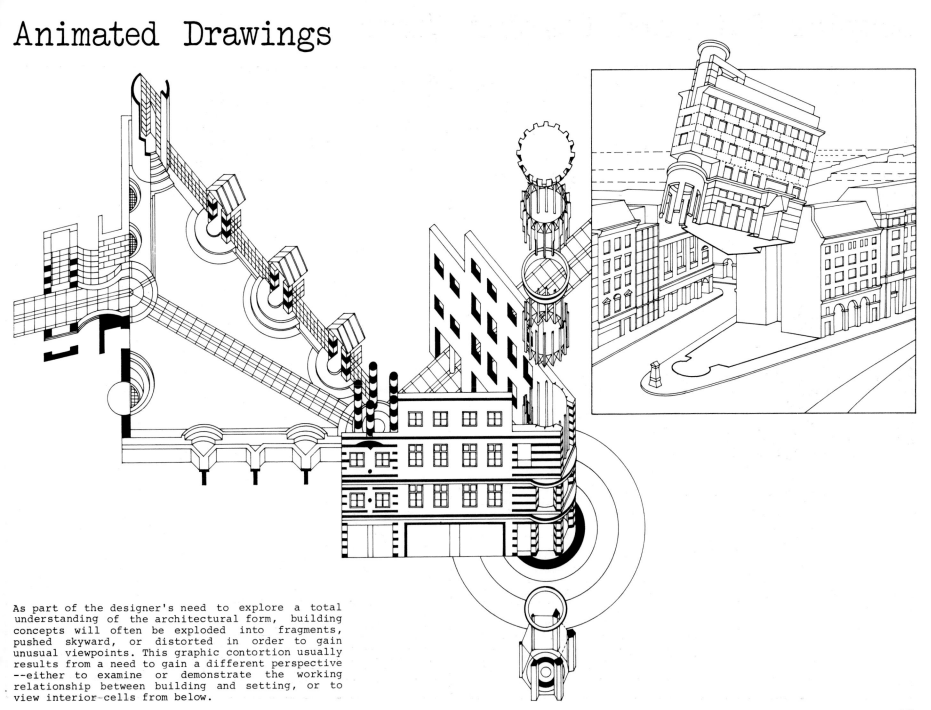

As part of the designer's need to explore a total understanding of the architectural form, building concepts will often be exploded into fragments, pushed skyward, or distorted in order to gain unusual viewpoints. This graphic contortion usually results from a need to gain a different perspective --either to examine or demonstrate the working relationship between building and setting, or to view interior cells from below.

# Symbols for Openings: Doors

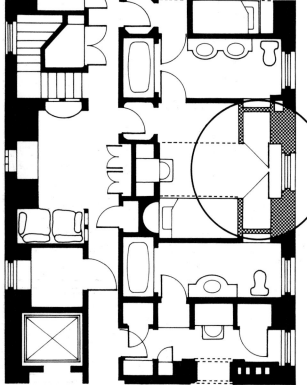

Symbols appear in the sectional cut of the external and partition walls of plans to denote the location, type, and function of openings. For example, a single-leaf, single-action door is always represented in an open position. Its leaf is shown at right angles to the closed position together with linear evidence of the arc of its swing. In describing the actual function of the door swing, this representation is preferred to the occasional and alternative use of a 45-degree line.

The various types and functions of doors are similarly represented in the plan view: single leaf, double action (a); double leaf, single action (b); double leaf, double action (c); double leaf, opposing action (d); folding or accordian door, center hung (f); recess hung sliding or pocket door (g); sliding door, face hung (h); and revolving door (i).

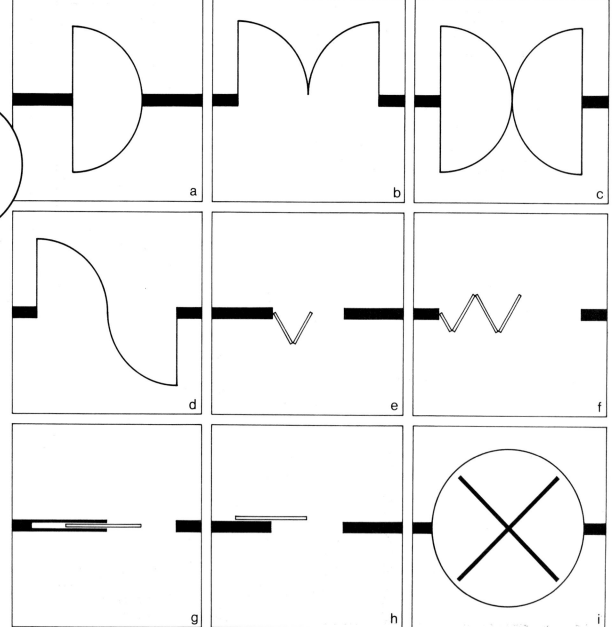

# Symbols for Openings: Windows

Depending upon the scale of the drawing, the portrayal of glass in plan windows can range from depiction by a single line to two lines that define the inner and outer plane of its thickness. Occasionally, within large-scale design plans, the type and opening capability of a window can be described.

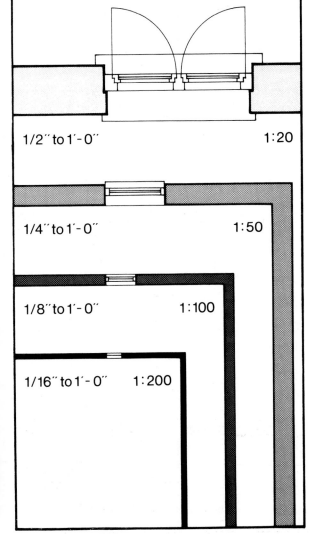

1/2″ to 1′-0″      1:20

1/4″ to 1′-0″      1:50

1/8″ to 1′-0″      1:100

1/16″ to 1′-0″      1:200

Two lines within a window seen in elevation form a triangle that symbolizes windows that swing open--its apex pointing to the side that is hinged. Pivoting windows are indicated with a cross--pivot points being shown with a dash. Sliding windows are signified by arrows that simply point in the direction of their action.

N.B.: Elevation window symbols are not usually included in design drawings, but this information is useful since, apart from introducing the various types of window opening, it also becomes useful when preparing production drawings at the later design stage.

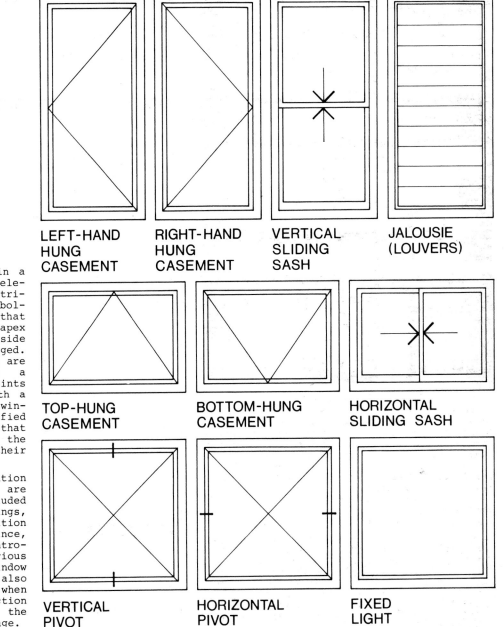

LEFT-HAND HUNG CASEMENT

RIGHT-HAND HUNG CASEMENT

VERTICAL SLIDING SASH

JALOUSIE (LOUVERS)

TOP-HUNG CASEMENT

BOTTOM-HUNG CASEMENT

HORIZONTAL SLIDING SASH

VERTICAL PIVOT

HORIZONTAL PIVOT

FIXED LIGHT

# Symbols for Staircases, Ramps, and Elevators

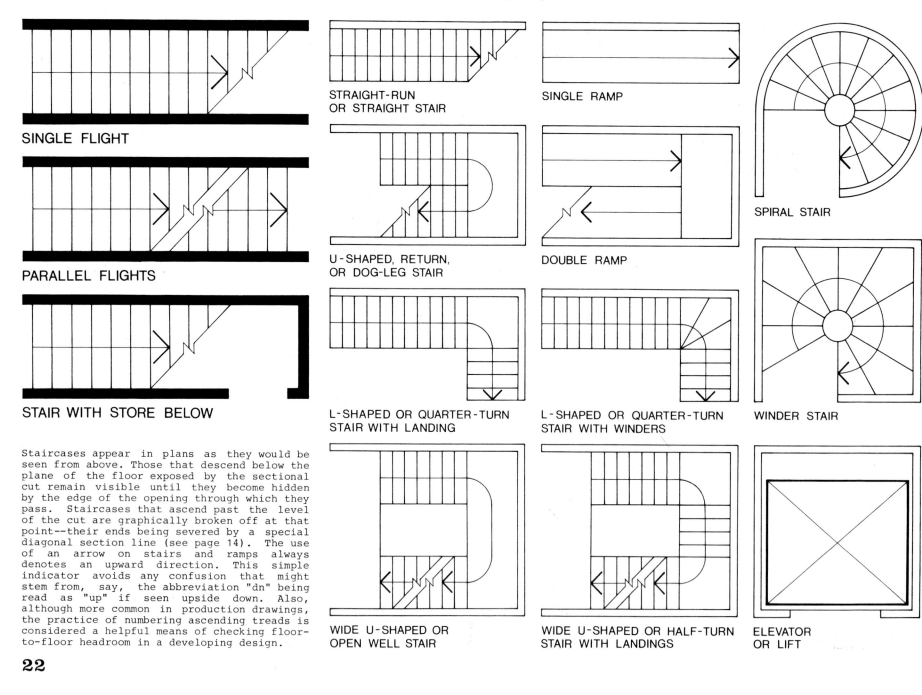

SINGLE FLIGHT

PARALLEL FLIGHTS

STAIR WITH STORE BELOW

STRAIGHT-RUN
OR STRAIGHT STAIR

U-SHAPED, RETURN,
OR DOG-LEG STAIR

L-SHAPED OR QUARTER-TURN
STAIR WITH LANDING

WIDE U-SHAPED OR
OPEN WELL STAIR

SINGLE RAMP

DOUBLE RAMP

L-SHAPED OR QUARTER-TURN
STAIR WITH WINDERS

WIDE U-SHAPED OR HALF-TURN
STAIR WITH LANDINGS

SPIRAL STAIR

WINDER STAIR

ELEVATOR
OR LIFT

Staircases appear in plans as they would be seen from above. Those that descend below the plane of the floor exposed by the sectional cut remain visible until they become hidden by the edge of the opening through which they pass. Staircases that ascend past the level of the cut are graphically broken off at that point--their ends being severed by a special diagonal section line (see page 14). The use of an arrow on stairs and ramps always denotes an upward direction. This simple indicator avoids any confusion that might stem from, say, the abbreviation "dn" being read as "up" if seen upside down. Also, although more common in production drawings, the practice of numbering ascending treads is considered a helpful means of checking floor-to-floor headroom in a developing design.

# Northpoints and Graphic Scales

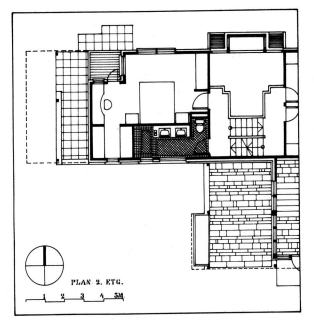

PLAN 2. ETG.

A convention in both building and site plans is that they are always drafted with north occurring at the top of the drawing. Northpoints should be clearly positioned in conjunction with the plan, their design the prerogative of the designer (see page 128). Here we illustrate a variety of the more unambiguous examples.

The graphic representation of the scale used for a design drawing is an important device, especially when the drawing is to be reproduced and resized. The graphic evidence of the scale then allows the dimensions of the drawing to be readable at whatever the reduction or enlargement. However, whenever a drawn scale is used, its proportional units of linear measurement should be clearly and simply stated. Here are a few examples of graphic scales--including versions showing both feet and meters--found in orthographics.

N.B.: As both the northpoint and the scale occur outside the plan, it is important to treat them as compositional elements of the overall drawing format.

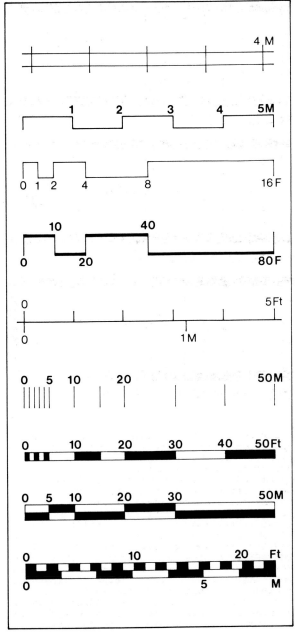

# Codes for Materials (U.S.)

TYP. S. ENTRY EXT. WALL
CONSTRUCTION :

SYNTHETIC PLASTER
MATERIAL ON 2" RIG. INSUL.
ON PLYWD SHEATHING ON
2 × 6's @ 16" O.C. w/
5 1/2" BATT. INSUL.

PLAN DETAIL

## Section

## Elevation

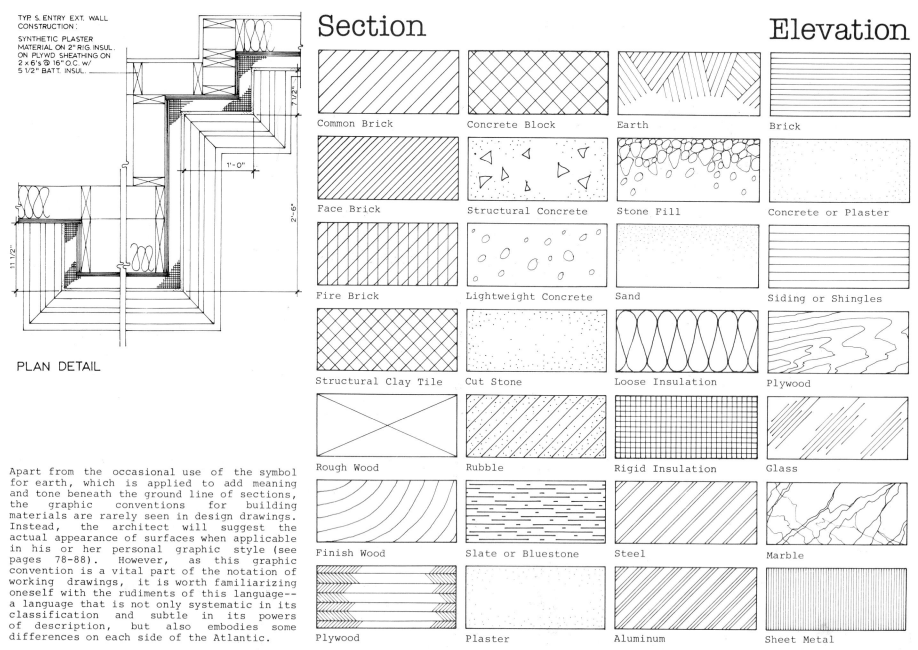

| Section | | | Elevation |
|---|---|---|---|
| Common Brick | Concrete Block | Earth | Brick |
| Face Brick | Structural Concrete | Stone Fill | Concrete or Plaster |
| Fire Brick | Lightweight Concrete | Sand | Siding or Shingles |
| Structural Clay Tile | Cut Stone | Loose Insulation | Plywood |
| Rough Wood | Rubble | Rigid Insulation | Glass |
| Finish Wood | Slate or Bluestone | Steel | Marble |
| Plywood | Plaster | Aluminum | Sheet Metal |

Apart from the occasional use of the symbol for earth, which is applied to add meaning and tone beneath the ground line of sections, the graphic conventions for building materials are rarely seen in design drawings. Instead, the architect will suggest the actual appearance of surfaces when applicable in his or her personal graphic style (see pages 78-88). However, as this graphic convention is a vital part of the notation of working drawings, it is worth familiarizing oneself with the rudiments of this language-- a language that is not only systematic in its classification and subtle in its powers of description, but also embodies some differences on each side of the Atlantic.

**24**

# Codes for Materials (U.K.)

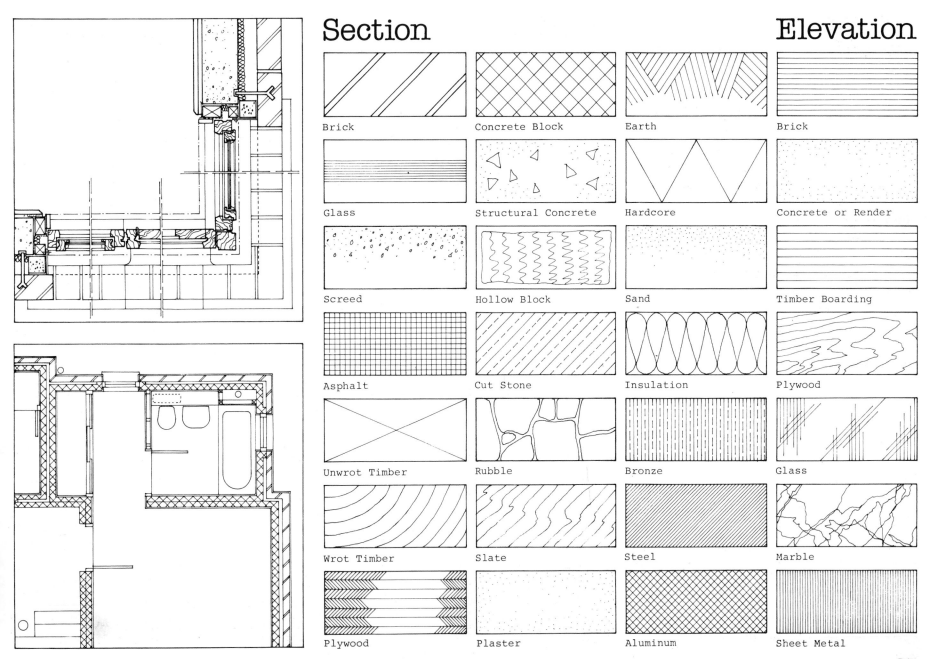

## Section

Brick

Glass

Screed

Asphalt

Unwrot Timber

Wrot Timber

Plywood

Concrete Block

Structural Concrete

Hollow Block

Cut Stone

Rubble

Slate

Plaster

Earth

Hardcore

Sand

Insulation

Bronze

Steel

Aluminum

## Elevation

Brick

Concrete or Render

Timber Boarding

Plywood

Glass

Marble

Sheet Metal

# Contours in Site Plans

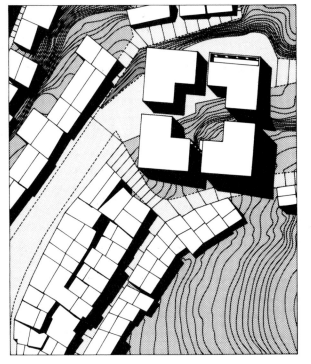

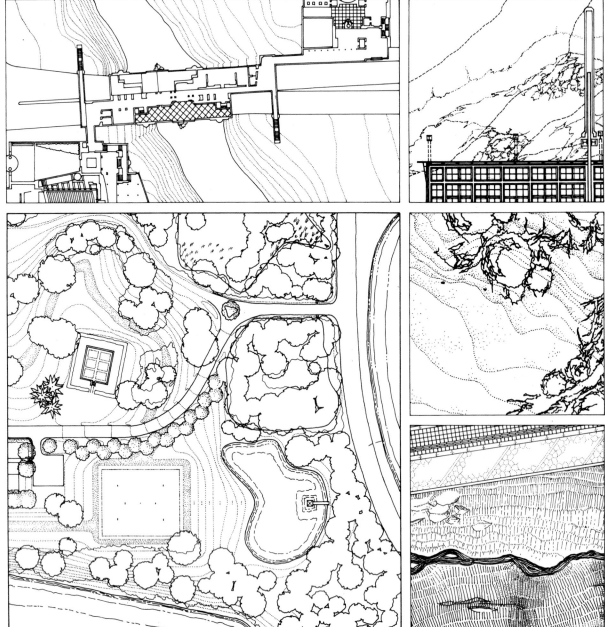

Contour lines in both site and landscape plans are a graphic convention for describing topographical changes in the surface of the landscape. Contours represent imaginary lines that symbolize a constant height above sea level or another reference datum and trace the elevation of that height in a continuous manner. When reading contour plans, the direction of each line informs on the sectioned shape of the landmass at that elevation. The distance between each contour line indicates the degree of undulation in the site. For example, contour lines close together indicate a steep incline; those far apart describe a terrain that is relatively flat.

The contour convention can be shown in different ways: continuous lines, broken lines, and chains of dots. When a tonal rendition is required, hatching can be applied that models the terrain by simulating their vertical profiles. Another option is to apply value progressions of wash to each successive contour from dark to light as they "climb" toward the viewer.

# Existing and Proposed

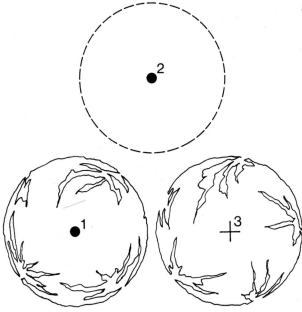

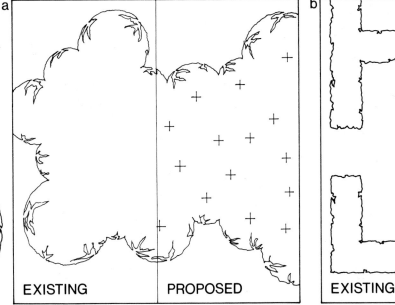

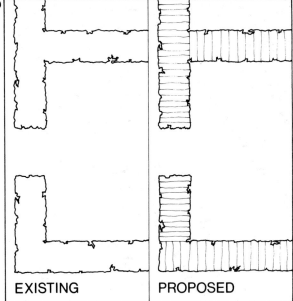

EXISTING    PROPOSED

EXISTING    PROPOSED

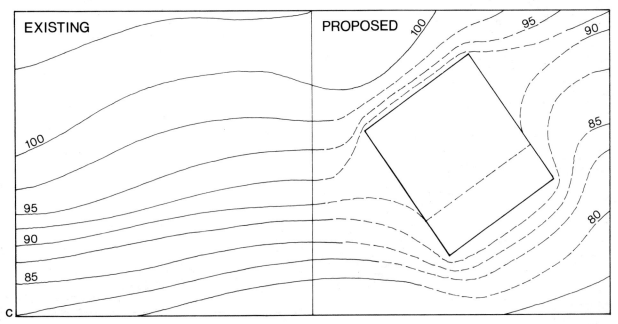

EXISTING    PROPOSED

A further dimension of the orthographic codes for plans is the ability to differentiate between existing and proposed events. For example, the three plan views of a tree (above) show three different intentions: the first records an existing tree (1), the second indicates an existing tree that is to be removed (2), and the third indicates a proposed new tree (3). Similarly, woodland areas can be shown as existing or proposed using the same code (a), but proposed hedge-rows are indicated by the introduction of a series of fine lines drawn across their mass (b). By contrast, the difference between existing and proposed contours is simply the difference between a continuous line and a dashed line (c).

# Shadow Conventions

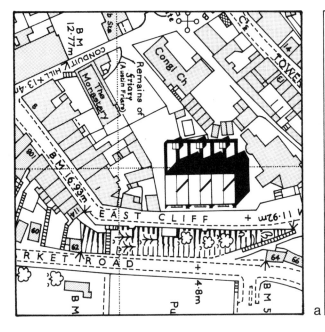

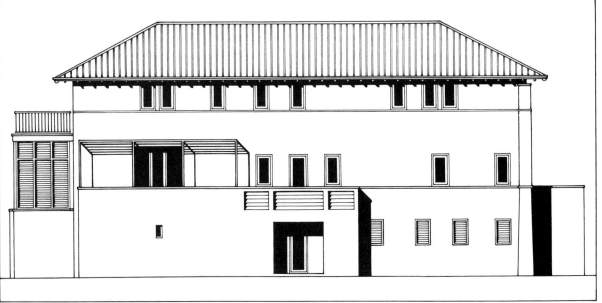

a

The convention for shadows in plans sees the direction of the sun's rays as entering the drawing from the bottom-left corner, i.e., over the viewer's left shoulder, at an angle of 45 degrees. Meanwhile, the shadow convention for elevations and sections finds sunlight projected down from the upper-left corner and across the drawing at a 45-degree angle. Site plans (above) and elevations (a) and roof plans (b) project the full extent of cast shadows, but floor plans and sections (c) project a length of shadow corresponding to the respective height or depth of the slice.

N.B.: When necessary, these directional conventions can be broken. However, the main reason for inserting shadows in orthographics is to test the impact of light and shadow on the space surrounding or contained by the building design. Furthermore, by exposing flat and featureless facades, shadow projection in elevations acts as a check on the three-dimensional quality of a design proposal (shadow projection methods are described in chapter four).

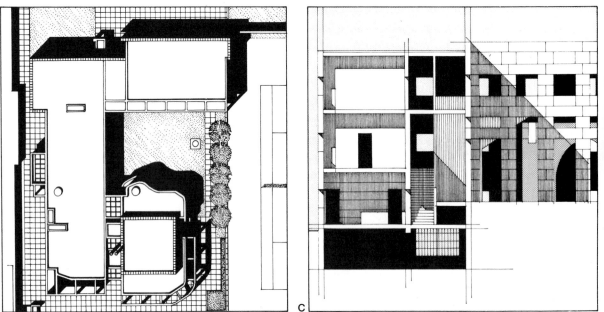

b

c

# 2 FLOORSCAPE, GROUNDSCAPE, AND TREES

# Floorscape

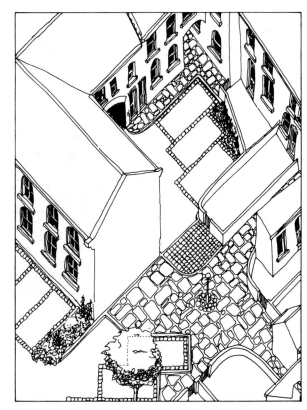

Together with planting, the hard surface of floorscape treatments of pathways, patios, piazzas, etc., will often register as a positive and detailed element of landscape and site plans. For instance, walkways are often shown with delineated modules to illustrate both the makeup of their surface and the pattern of circulation systems within the site. When not fully drawn, hard floorscape areas can be hinted at--either by selectively drawing areas of joints around their perimeter, or by detailing exclusively within the areas of shadow projected from adjacent wall planes. In simultaneously fulfilling two graphic roles, the latter technique is both economical and convincing. However, as with all graphic depictions of surface materials, a conviction begins with a working knowledge of the different pattern-making options as well as how the individual units fit within the overall pattern and how they form edges.

## Brick

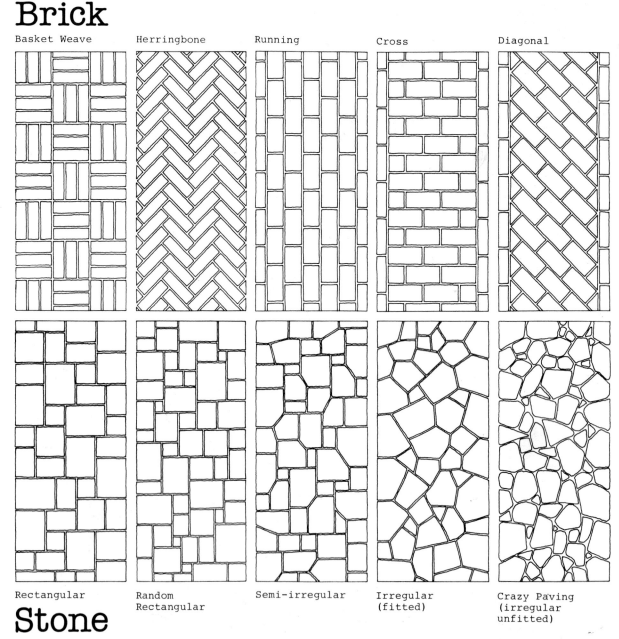

Basket Weave   Herringbone   Running   Cross   Diagonal

Rectangular   Random Rectangular   Semi-irregular   Irregular (fitted)   Crazy Paving (irregular unfitted)

## Stone

# Floorscape

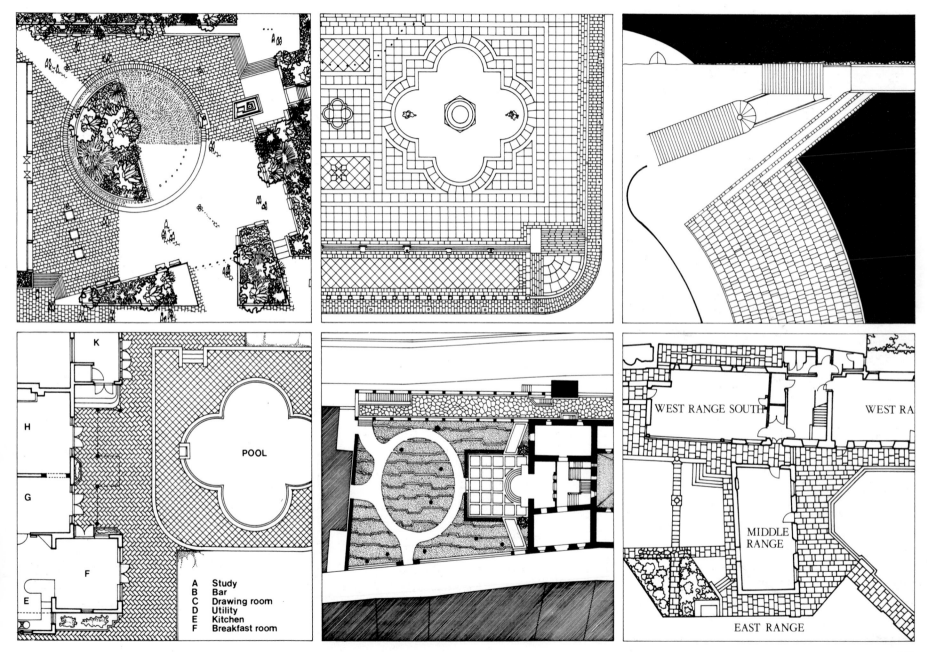

A   Study
B   Bar
C   Drawing room
D   Utility
E   Kitchen
F   Breakfast room

POOL

WEST RANGE SOUTH

WEST RA

MIDDLE
RANGE

EAST RANGE

# Ground Cover and Shrubbery

In small-scale plans, the rendition of groundscape can resort to one of a range of controlled short-stroke textural techniques. Shrubbery, on the other hand, is delineated in outline. When drawn at a greater scale, this textural indication of surface cover can be economically suggested by its confinement to the periphery of large areas--this suggestion tending to be filled in by the eye. Also at these scales, a successful depiction of shrubbery avoids a meaningless and distracting scribble. The degree of freedom of foliage outline will reflect the degree of landscape formality suggested by the design. Also, when it assumes prominence in the foreground of perspectives it can, as exemplified by the drawings shown on page 33, take on a positive and well-drawn role in the overall composition.

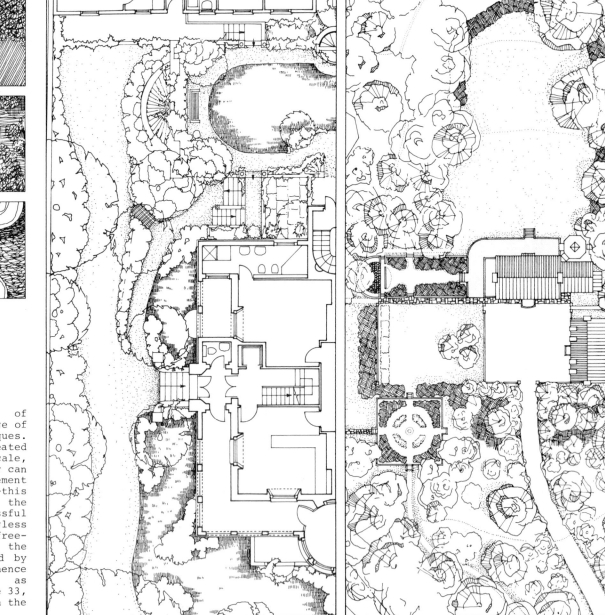

# Ground Cover and Shrubbery

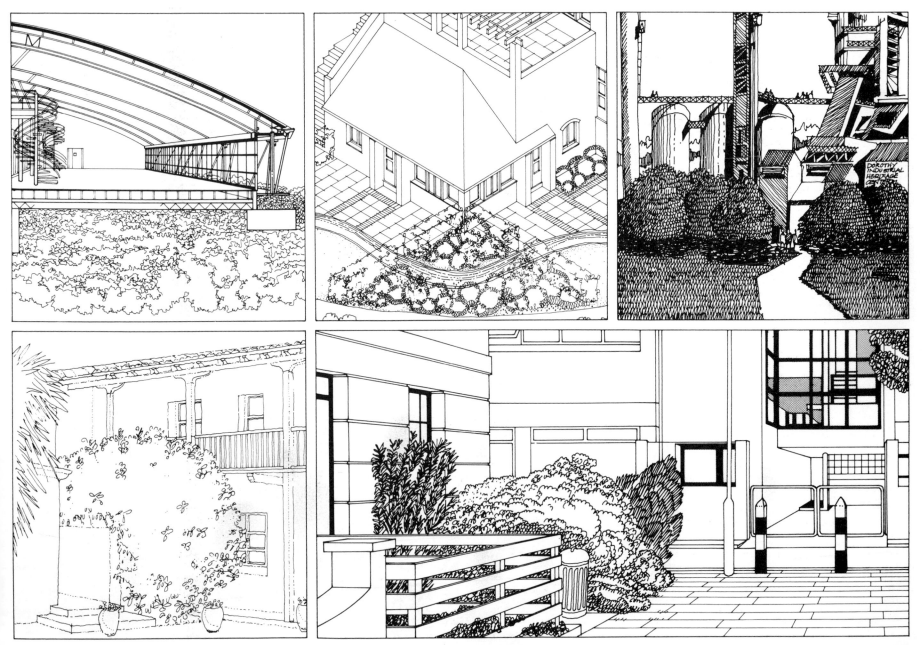

# Trees in Plans

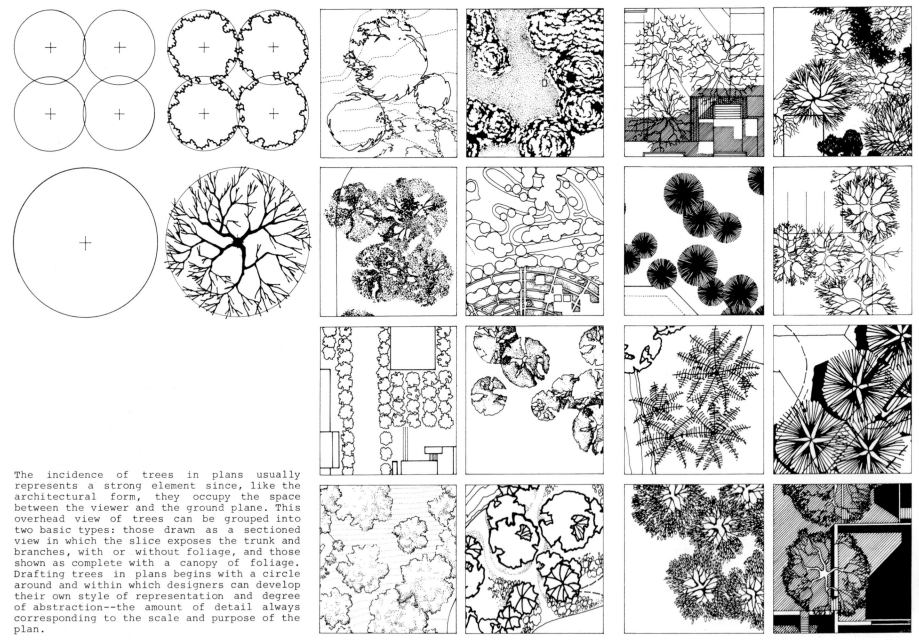

The incidence of trees in plans usually represents a strong element since, like the architectural form, they occupy the space between the viewer and the ground plane. This overhead view of trees can be grouped into two basic types: those drawn as a sectioned view in which the slice exposes the trunk and branches, with or without foliage, and those shown as complete with a canopy of foliage. Drafting trees in plans begins with a circle around and within which designers can develop their own style of representation and degree of abstraction--the amount of detail always corresponding to the scale and purpose of the plan.

# Trees in Plans

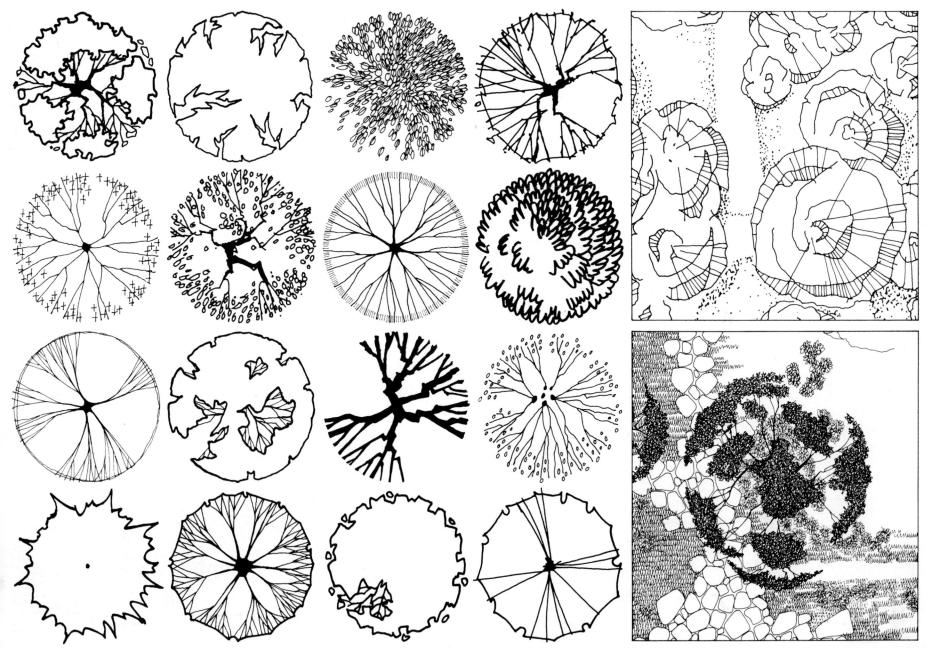

# How to Draw Trees

A graphic understanding of trees is rooted in their experience through sketchbook studies. Trees should be sketched at different points in the year so that both their skeletal and foliated structures can be studied. In this way, their basic form and botanical detail can be examined in the same fashion that you might study the anatomy of the human figure. This activity will not only help you to understand their growth patterns, but it will also enable you to draw the characteristics of specific species in relation to their setting.

When sketching, first determine the overall shape and proportion of trunk to mass of foliage--noting the shapes left between the mass of leaves.

**1**

**2**

Sketchbook studies can then be simplified for inclusion in design drawings--this form of direct observation avoiding the banality of the stereotype and giving a greater sense of presence to the resulting graphic.

N.B.: Proposed trees are usually depicted as mature specimens in architectural drawings.

**3** Many leading designers have developed their own personal and distinctive techniques for showing trees in their graphics. The simply drawn specimens below reflect those developed by Romaldo Giurgola and Le Corbusier, respectively.

# Conifer Tree Types

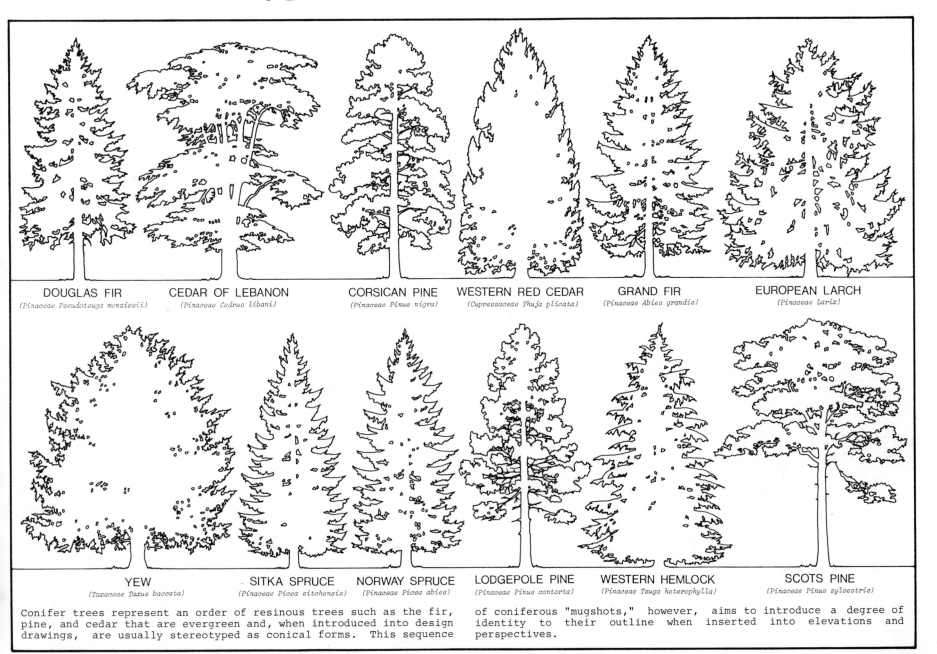

DOUGLAS FIR
*(Pinaceae Pseudotsuga menziesii)*

CEDAR OF LEBANON
*(Pinaceae Cedrus libani)*

CORSICAN PINE
*(Pinaceae Pinus nigra)*

WESTERN RED CEDAR
*(Cupressaceae Thuja plicata)*

GRAND FIR
*(Pinaceae Abies grandis)*

EUROPEAN LARCH
*(Pinaceae Larix)*

YEW
*(Taxaceae Taxus baccata)*

SITKA SPRUCE
*(Pinaceae Picea sitchensis)*

NORWAY SPRUCE
*(Pinaceae Picea abies)*

LODGEPOLE PINE
*(Pinaceae Pinus contorta)*

WESTERN HEMLOCK
*(Pinaceae Tsuga heterophylla)*

SCOTS PINE
*(Pinaceae Pinus sylvestris)*

Conifer trees represent an order of resinous trees such as the fir, pine, and cedar that are evergreen and, when introduced into design drawings, are usually stereotyped as conical forms. This sequence of coniferous "mugshots," however, aims to introduce a degree of identity to their outline when inserted into elevations and perspectives.

# Deciduous Tree Types

The seasonal metamorphosis of deciduous trees transforms a canopy of summer screening into a winter tracery of filtering branches. Although the majority of design drawings depict deciduous trees in leaf, they can occasionally be found in elevations, paralines, and perspectives in a winter delineation. Therefore, this identity parade illustrates a selection of characteristic, mature species in both their summer and winter forms.

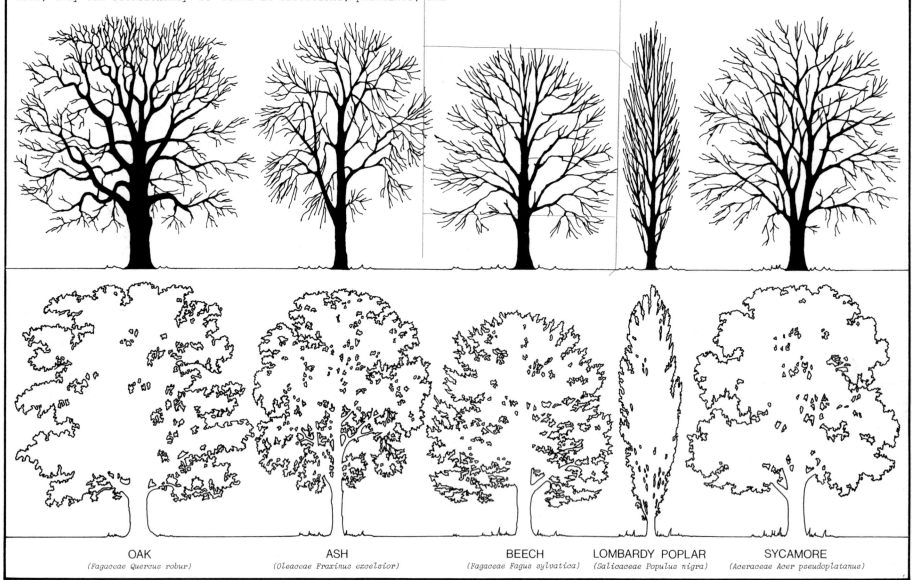

**OAK**
*(Fagaceae Quercus robur)*

**ASH**
*(Oleaceae Fraxinus excelsior)*

**BEECH**
*(Fagaceae Fagus sylvatica)*

**LOMBARDY POPLAR**
*(Salicaceae Populus nigra)*

**SYCAMORE**
*(Aceraceae Acer pseudoplatanus)*

# Deciduous Tree Types

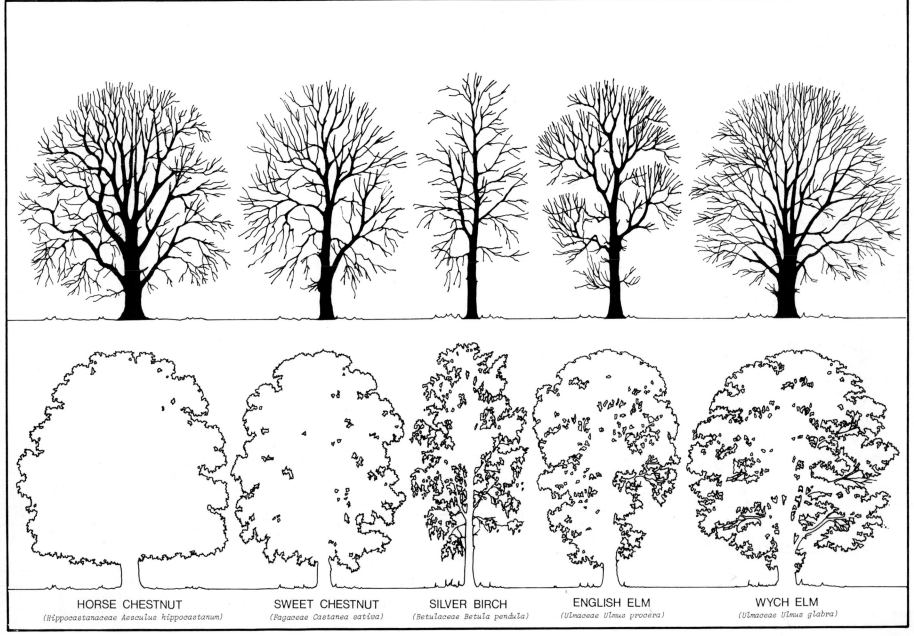

**HORSE CHESTNUT**
*(Hippocastanaceae Aesculus hippocastanum)*

**SWEET CHESTNUT**
*(Fagaceae Castanea sativa)*

**SILVER BIRCH**
*(Betulaceae Betula pendula)*

**ENGLISH ELM**
*(Ulmaceae Ulmus procera)*

**WYCH ELM**
*(Ulmaceae Ulmus glabra)*

# Palm Trees

The image of the palm tree tends to evoke a sense of the exotic and, as such, appears extensively in architectural drawings. Palm trees are often used as focal points fronting public buildings and inside the artificial climates of atriums, leisure centers, etc. Their popularity in architectural drawings is also probably due to the fact that, apart from being easy and pleasurable to draw, their frondlike silhouettes create a delicate counterpoint to the hard edge of building designs. Here are two popular species--the Washington filifera and the Pheonix dactylifera, respectively--followed by examples appearing in the work of different designers.

# Palm Trees

# Tree Groups in Elevations

These details, taken from a series of elevation drawings, demonstrate the effect of groups of trees in relation to the scale of buildings. Notice that in each case the line used to portray foliage brings a lively contrast to the hardline of the architectural form. In being proportionally sensitive to the relationship between trunk and canopy, the line describing foliage can be playful, fluid, intermittent, and, in some cases, sketchy. An additional aspect of these drawings is the variety of tree stylization. Differences in the level of objectivity possibly results from a corresponding degree of intimacy between designer and the site.

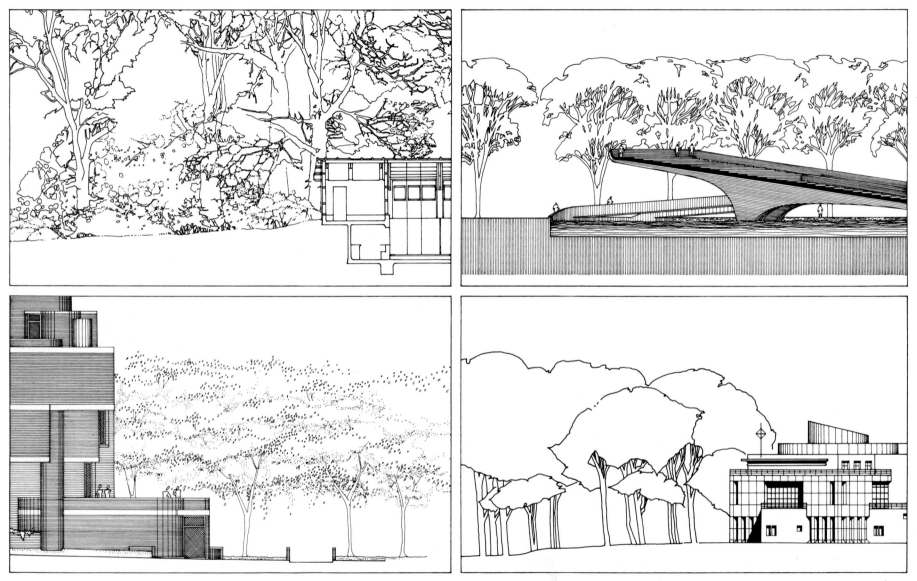

# Specimen Trees in Elevations

When dealing with sites that already contain mature trees, design drawings, such as elevations and sections, will feature them as having direct impact on the building design. In these cases, the tree becomes more fully developed graphically and will often be worked directly from an on-site photograph. This sequence of drawings exemplify such trees occupying the space between the viewer and the facade. In each case, the tree exists as a positive form, and in making no attempt to play a subservient role, it demands equal attention with the facade.

# Transparent Trees

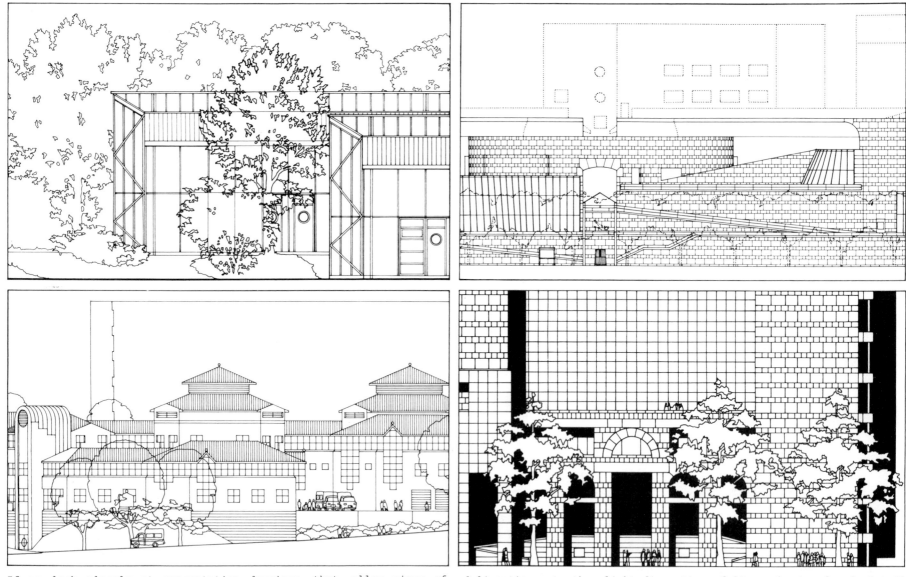

If we look closely at presentation drawings that allow views of architectural detail through a mass of trees, we find an extensive range of subtly different techniques used to achieve this transparency. These range from, among others, the obvious convention of broken-line foliage superimposed on the continuous line of facade delineation, to the slight disruption of lines showing facade detail behind the continuous line of foliage, to the careful arrangement of clusters of leaves so that a continuity of architectural detail is maintained.

# Transparent Trees

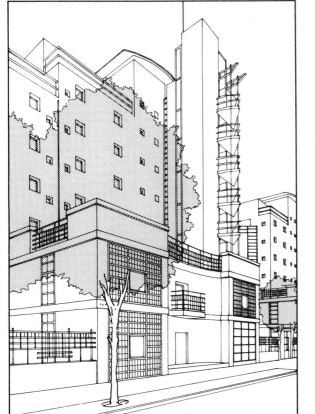

Culled from a variety of architects' perspectives and elevations, these details exemplify further variations on the transparency theme. For instance, an alternative technique involves the use of transparent film tone or watercolor wash to indicate foliage, while another technique reverses canopies delineated by a broken line by using this convention to indicate the facade as seen through the tree. Whichever technique you use, however, will depend upon the required degree of tree foliage intervention between viewer and facade.

# Trees in Axonometrics

In simulating an aerial and three-quarter view of objects, the axonometric depiction of trees is not as difficult as it, at first, might seem. For example, this tree has been isolated from an axonometric by O. M. Ungers. However, when placed into the context of its projection drawing setting, the tree --although appearing as an elevation in its isolated state --exists comfortably in the overhead view represented by the paraline drawing.

**1**

Therefore, trees destined for axonometric and isometric drawings require little modification. Basic differences between their elevational and overhead view refer to a fullness of canopy suggested in tonal drawings together with a slightly foreshortened view of the trunk.

**2**

The basic "circle-on-a-stick" form is a good starting point. Foliage is then introduced using a meandering line that, being sensitive to the scale of the recipient drawing, describes the soft edge of the canopy.

**3**

**4**

Trees are quickly drafted into different types of group formations, such as irregular, as in a copse, or formally, as in an avenue. In fact, many axonometric drawings introduce trees as they would appear in plans, i.e., minus trunks, such as in the detail from the Comprehensive Design Partnership (c) in which examples of both plan and three-dimensional views coexist in an acceptable manner.

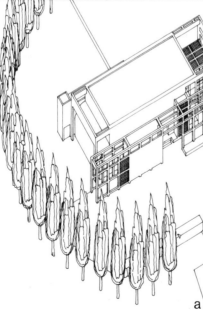

a

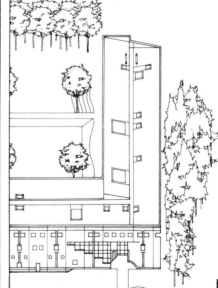

b

c

# Trees in Axonometrics

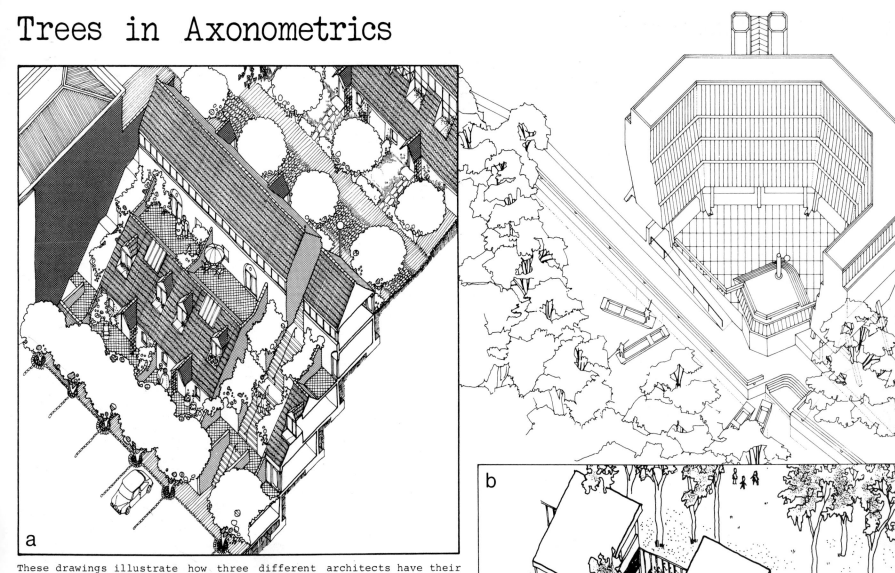

a

b

c

These drawings illustrate how three different architects have their own personal style for drawing the axonometric view of trees. The approach used by Napper Collerton reduces the form to a repeated stereotype--any variation being expressed in tiny glimpses through the mass of foliage (a). Another approach is Walter Segal's distinctively fluid and sketchy style, which uses a hint of tone and a nervous outline to create a more natural-looking tree (b). The third drawing, taken from the work of Jim Stirling, translates the tree mass into a sequence of overlapping and layered clumps of foliage (c). This approach--beautifully illustrated by the lower-right tree-- provides a highly successful technique for developing convincing axonometric tree forms.

# Tree or Building as Center of Attention

**1**

A basic decision concerning the inclusion of trees in design drawings, particularly in axonometrics, is whether they or the building design will function as the center of attention. For example, when the building is intended as the central role in the message of the drawing, surrounding trees are usually represented as a simple outline drawing to describe their location, size, and landscape function.

**2**

Conversely, when the landscape setting rather than the building becomes the salient message of the drawing, trees tend to be portrayed more literally, with the detail of foliage providing a value contrast with the delineated built form.

**3**

Obviously, a third variation on this decision is to render both the building design and its attendant landscape elements in a similar technique and to the same degree of value and detail. By creating a more balanced impression, this decision leads to describing the impact of a built form on its setting. The drawings on this page are based on extracts of the work of Franco Purini & Laura Thermes, Rodrigo Pérez de Arce, and Terry Farrell, respectively.

# Tree Techniques for Wooded Areas

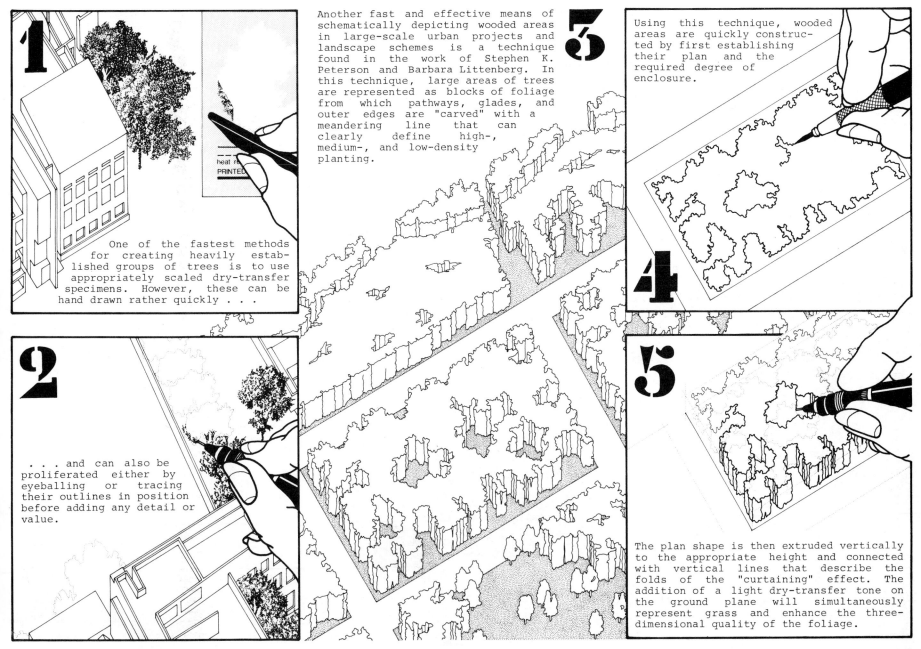

**1**

One of the fastest methods for creating heavily established groups of trees is to use appropriately scaled dry-transfer specimens. However, these can be hand drawn rather quickly . . .

**2**

. . . and can also be proliferated either by eyeballing or tracing their outlines in position before adding any detail or value.

Another fast and effective means of schematically depicting wooded areas in large-scale urban projects and landscape schemes is a technique found in the work of Stephen K. Peterson and Barbara Littenberg. In this technique, large areas of trees are represented as blocks of foliage from which pathways, glades, and outer edges are "carved" with a meandering line that can clearly define high-, medium-, and low-density planting.

**3**

Using this technique, wooded areas are quickly constructed by first establishing their plan and the required degree of enclosure.

**4**

**5**

The plan shape is then extruded vertically to the appropriate height and connected with vertical lines that describe the folds of the "curtaining" effect. The addition of a light dry-transfer tone on the ground plane will simultaneously represent grass and enhance the three-dimensional quality of the foliage.

# Planting on Buildings

The insertion of plants and trees on the roofs and balconies of elevations is often used as a graphic afterthought to soften the impact of building designs. Sometimes referred to as giving a design the "green slime treatment," this application can involve several techniques, from the banality of a dotted line haze or a "dripping wax" outline to simulate overhanging planting, to the introduction of highly detailed roof gardens that function to alter the skyline silhouette.

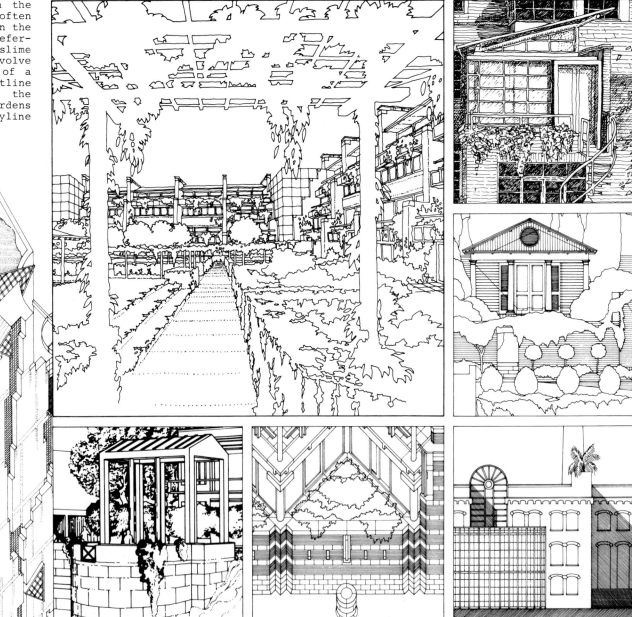

# Planting in Buildings

As with planting on or around the mass of a building design, interior planting often appears in sections and perspectives as a kind of afterthought. But instead of drawing these with abandon or reducing them to a scribbled presence, even a minimal depiction of identifiable species can strengthen the conviction of interior space. These details illustrate the designer's wish to explore the impact of plants on different proportions of interior volume. They also illustrate an important figural context in which an organic line representing foliage brings greater visual interest to the angularity of lines representing the architecture.

# Function of Trees in Design Drawings

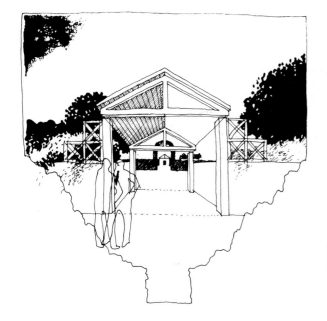

Whether shown as a concise silhouette or in some degree of detail, trees should be depicted in design drawings exactly the way they would appear in the landscape, i.e., acting individually or collectively to define, frame, and filter views. For example, foreground trees can appear simply by showing the underside of their canopies in the upper portion of a drawing to frame a view through to the design proposal. Or, the negative space between trees can be used to filter a view of the design proposal. Used with figures, trees can also heighten a sense of perspective by both exploiting distance in the horizontal plane and by any variation in their height or that of the ground plane. Finally, when used as backdrops, as in the illustration above, their foliage mass can act to complement the angular forms of an architectural structure.

# 3 FIGURES, FURNITURE, AND FEATURES

# Figures in Plans

Figures are rarely depicted in plans. This is because they are difficult to draw from the overhead perspective represented by the plan and also because their appearance from this unusual angle can overcomplicate the information projected by a small-scale plan. At the larger scales, however, some interior designers will occasionally populate their plans in order to reinforce spatial function. When this happens, the simple figures found on pressure transfer sheets are invariably used. These show scaled and diagrammatic bird's-eye views of people walking, carrying papers, and in postures for relaxing in chairs and sitting at tables. When used, such figures should be positioned so that, either individually or in small groups, they interact with rooms, doors, corridors, and so on.

# An Introduction to Figure Drawing

Generally speaking, the human figure rarely occurs in design drawings as a large and dominant element. Rather, figures tend to appear in small groups and crowds as a means of enhancing scale, endorsing functions, and imbuing drawings with a sense of activity and identity. However, this diminutive appearance of people in design graphics should not be a license to subject their representation to the banality of a "clothes peg" stereotype. Even at the smallest of scales, they should be abstracted and simplified against a working knowledge of the proportion of the human figure. Proportionally, the human body can be subdivided into $7\frac{1}{2}$ equal units; the head being the unit on which this subdivision is based.

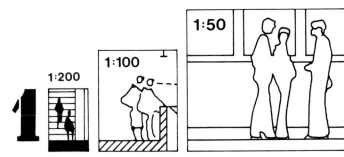

1:200  1:100  1:50

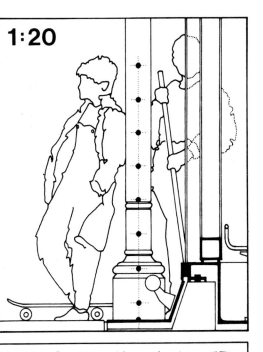

1:20

**2**

A common method of introducing figures into elevations and perspectives is to collect a file of photographs of people at different scales and in different postures, i.e., standing, walking, running, and sitting. These can be used as a source for tracing before their transfer onto artwork or, using a grid, rescaled into the required size of the recipient drawing.

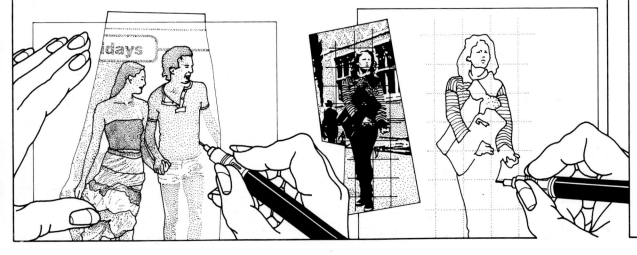

Another method of sketching people that is used by some designers is to purchase a manikin or an ergonome--a small-scale working model of a figure. The latter can be made by cutting its working parts from cardboard or plastic and jointed with paper fasteners. Once assembled, the ergonome can function as a portable model of human proportions that can assume any position and be used for making scaled drawings.

**3**

# Functions of Figures in Design Drawings

Apart from populating the space inside and around proposed architecture, the inclusion of figures can bring a greater reality to design drawings. Figures can be compositionally structured into overlapping groups to exploit spatial depth and be located to animate any changes in level. Most important is to avoid crowd hyperactivity and, whenever possible, to show figures interacting with the building. The details shown here, from a range of different scales and types of drawing, demonstrate such an interaction. The people here and on the facing page, simply drawn, stand, line up, walk, sit in conversational groups, climb stairs, point to features, lean over balconies, and generally participate in their environment.

# Figures in Elevations

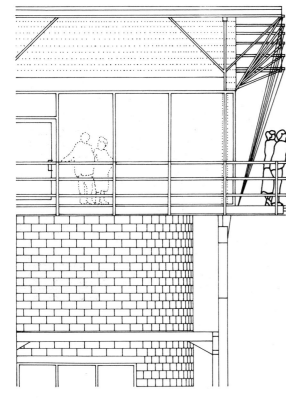

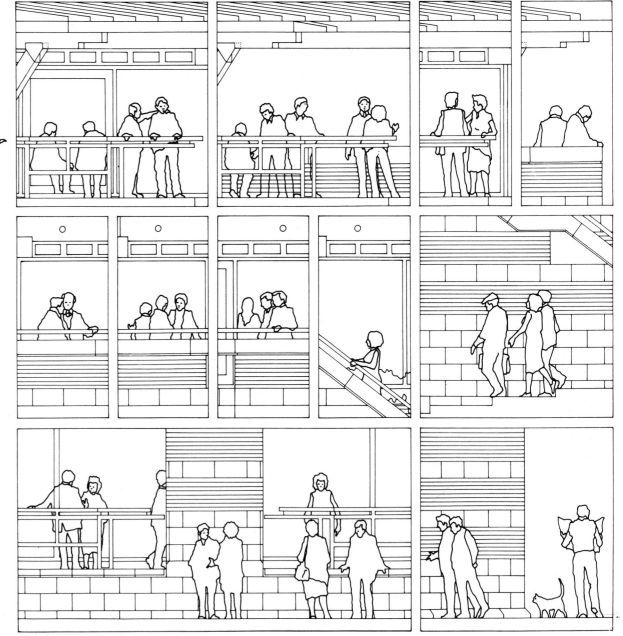

Using a basic understanding of the proportion of the human figure, graphic delineations can be used to good effect in elevations. Rather than an arbitrary placement, a direct inter-action with the space around building designs, or a direct contact with the structure, will give their presence a sense of purpose. For example, figures should be encouraged to occupy the center of entrances and corridors seen at right angles to the plane of the elevation. They should also be encouraged to touch the building either by leaning, holding, or sitting.

An added sense of occupation is given when, in larger scale elevations, figures can be observed both inside and outside the building, such as in the example above. Here, while those outside the elevation are shown in a continuous outline, the existence of people behind glass is suggested using the broken line device.

# Figures in Sections

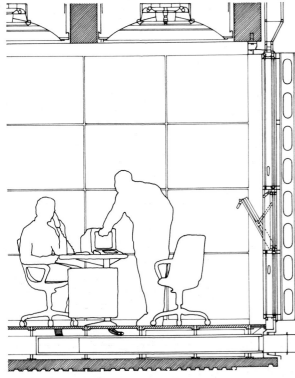

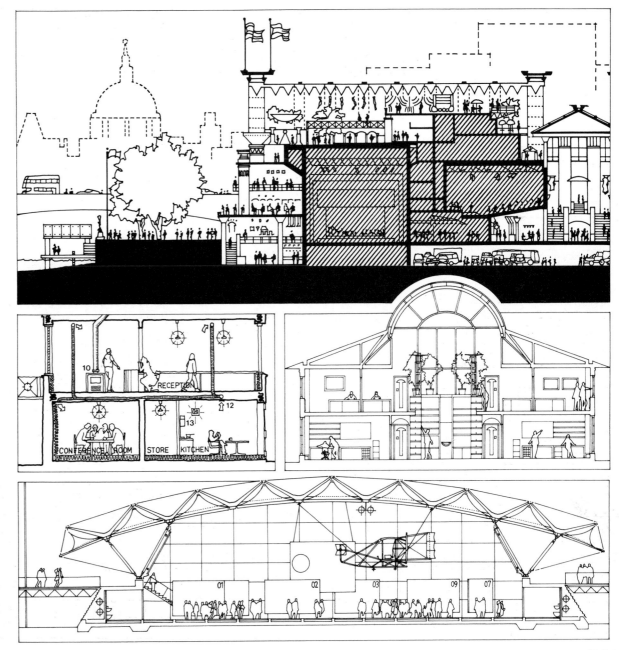

Figures in sections appear exactly as those in elevations except that, when located inside the sliced view of buildings, they tend to be less active. However, when interacting with interior features--such as furniture, shelving, windows, and doors--and, in general, when emphasizing function and creating a sense of place, the same progression of diminishing detail of figures along with the diminishing scale of drawings should be faithfully observed. As a rule, figures tend to be drafted in outline, but in some smaller scale sections they occasionally appear as black silhouettes when, if not drawn, they are selected from those on proprietary pressure transfer sheets. Although there are two examples in our gallery of details that show figures inhabiting the spaces of production sections, these are exceptions to the rule. This is because the use of figures in working drawings is usually avoided so as not to conflict with the constructional information contained within the sectional cut.

# Figures in Axonometrics

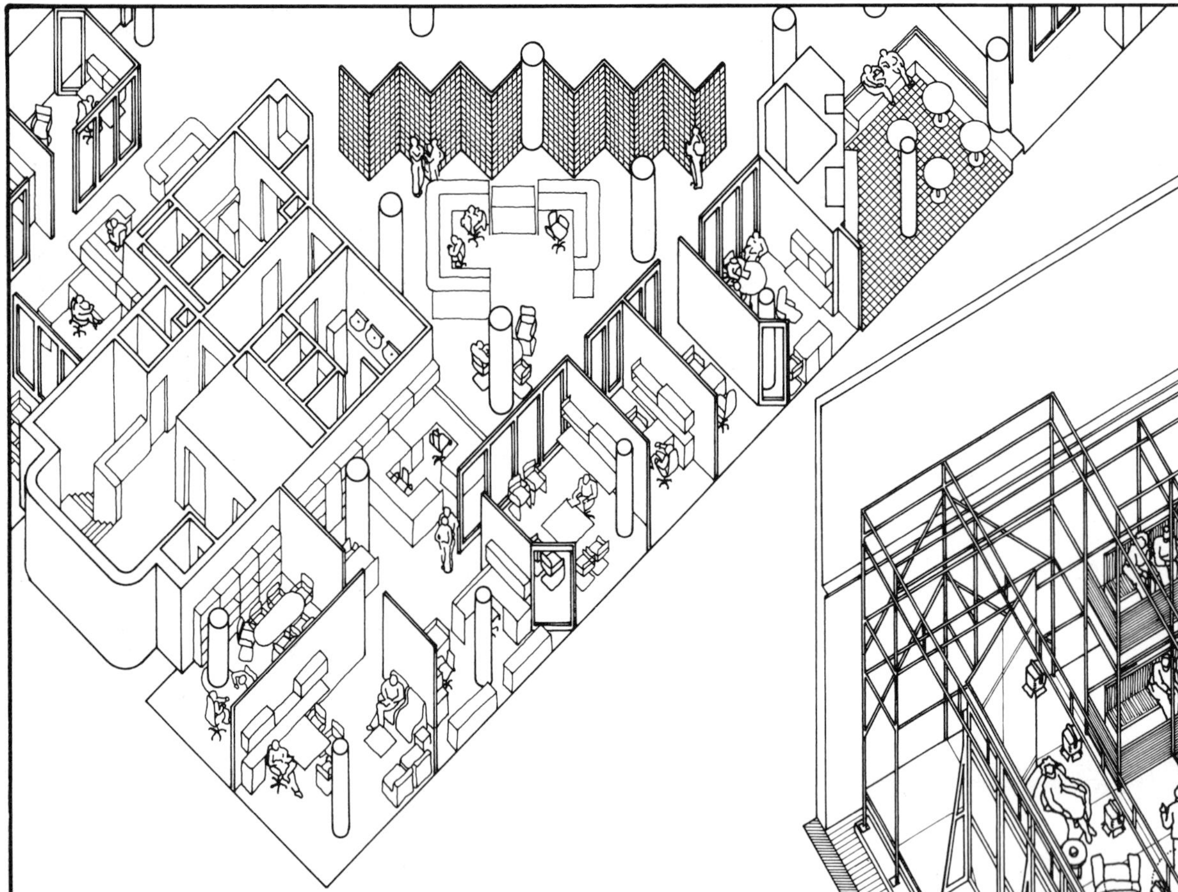

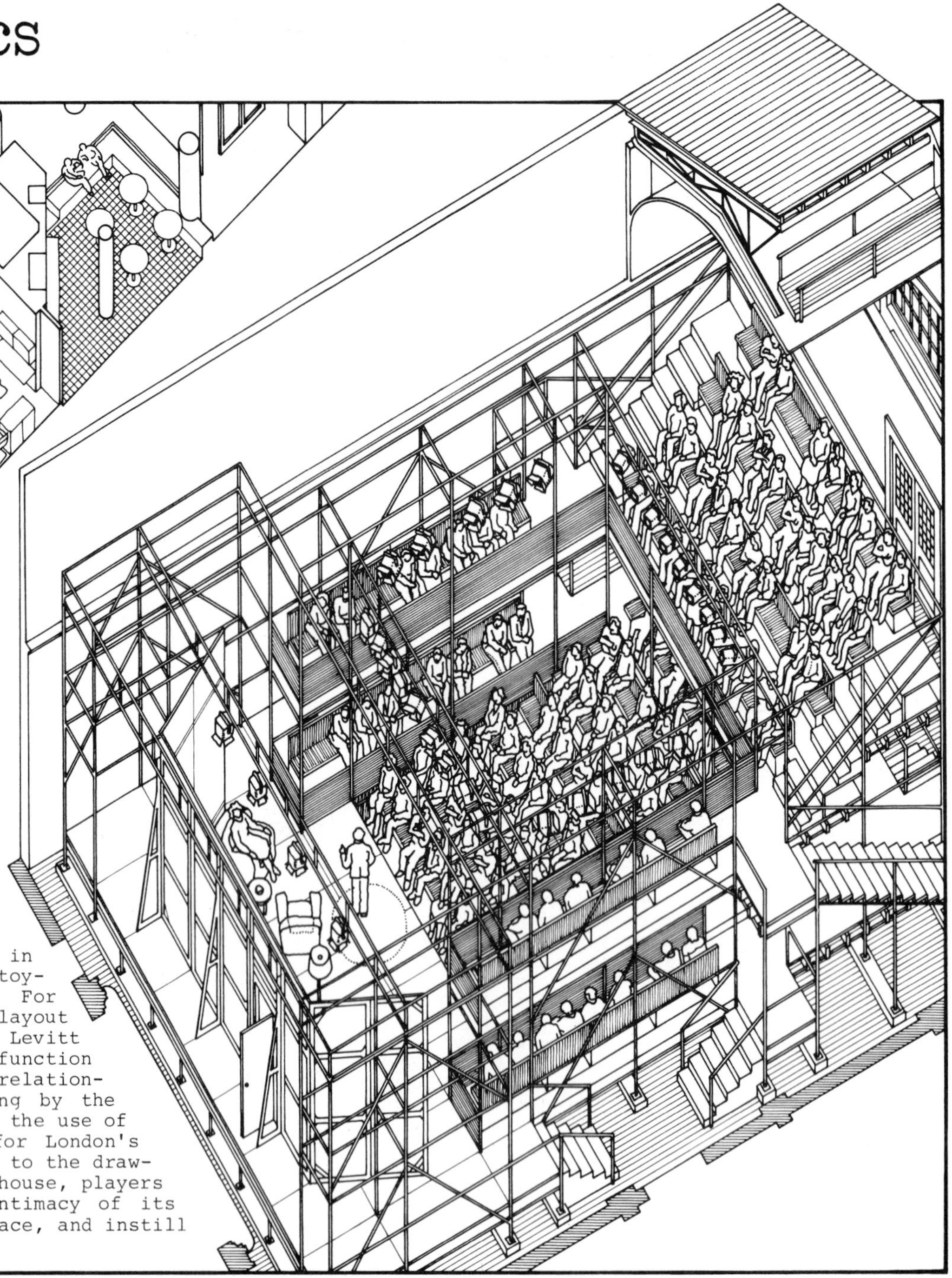

There is no doubt that the inclusion of human figures in axonometrics depicting interior spaces avoids a potential toy-town effect that can result from distortions in scale. For example, in the above drawing--a detail from an office layout design for a television station adapted from the work of Levitt Bernstein and Bruce Gorluck--the impression of volume and function of individual office layouts, together with their working relationship to overall planning, is instantly given greater meaning by the location and activity of its simply drawn occupants. Also, the use of 112 figures in Tim Foster's axonometric of his design for London's Tricycle Theater on the right brings a new level of meaning to the drawing. In depicting a performance playing to an almost-full house, players and audience establish a greater understanding of the intimacy of its scale, clarify the function of each layer of auditorium space, and instill a sense of occasion.

# Figures in Axonometrics

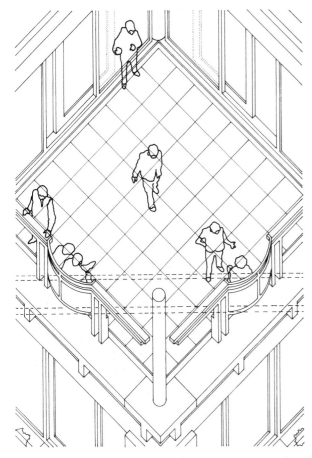

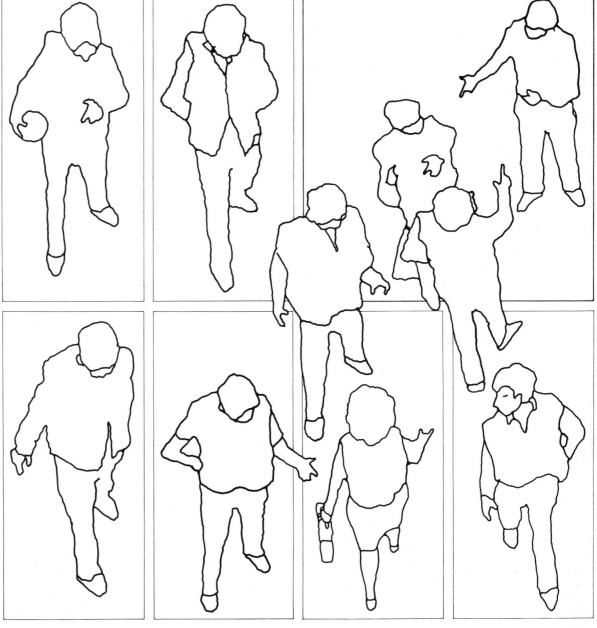

Unlike trees, the human figure requires some careful modification so that its appearance conforms to the distortion in the vertical plane when seen in axonometrics.

It is a good idea to start a file of figures for use in paraline drawings. The file could represent standing, walking, and sitting people who are drawn individually as well as formed into small groups. Initially, figure drawings can be outlined at a conveniently larger scale and, when required for use, be reduced on a photocopier to an appropriate size for their trace-transfer onto the recipient axonometric. This page illustrates a collection of axonometric figures developed by David Grindley of Denton Scott Associates.

# Figures in Perspectives

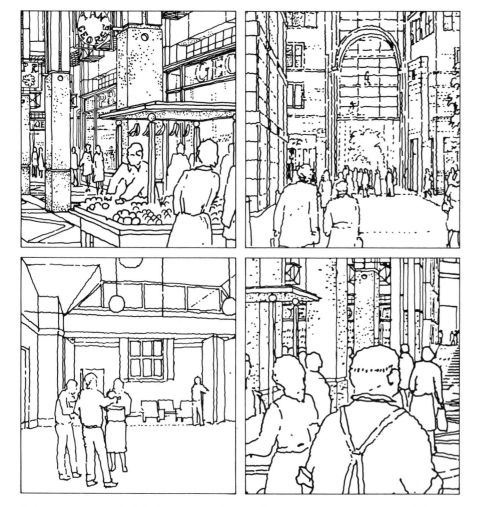

**2**

This sequence of details is redrawn from the perspectives of Robert Thompson. Their distinctive style results from a thick-penned and broken-line drawing technique that, in concerning itself with solidity and surface texture, presents architectural and human form as reduced to a minimum of linear information.

**1**

The apparent casual appearance of these drawings disguises a sophisticated and highly structured compositional deployment of figures in which groups of people constitute elements that animate space, complement building form, and, above all, exploit the depth of pictorial space. However, as the eye level of all the figures occupying a ground plane will coincide with the horizon line in a perspective drawn to be seen from normal height, their placement becomes a simple task, only their size and detail in relation to the depth of the implied space need be controlled. Establishing the relative sizes of figures in such perspectives is achieved by extending lines along the ground plane from the vanishing point into the foreground area. In conjunction with the horizon line, figures can then be positioned in scale at any required point along this line.

# Figures in Perspectives

a

b

c

The two sports hall interiors on the left make an interesting comparison because of the degree of stylization used in their figures. In the lower example (b), ice skaters are simply outlined while, on the end wall, the three ice hockey skaters are symbolically abstracted into the design of a supergraphic. In the upper example (a), however, an unusual reversal of stylization takes place. This is because the ceiling-mounted supergraphics that occupy the aerial foreground assume a realistic appearance and hang above hurdlers, gymnasts, and onlookers drawn in a highly abstracted and stereotyped form. These two drawings are derived from the Building Design Partnership (above) and from Norman Foster Associates (below).

The street scene (c) is taken from another perspective of a project from the practice of Norman Foster. Here, figures have been deployed to animate a pedestrian route using a line drawing that combines a container outline with contained lines that--depending upon the nearness of figure to viewer--selectively picks out shoes, shirt pattern, and even buttons and watchstrap. An attempt has been made in all the examples on this page to communicate the spaces as they would really be used. All the incorporated figures have been assembled as units to compose a group activity that is directly related to the function of each space. Furthermore, by allowing us to identify with them, they provide a means through which we can "participate" with the environment they inhabit although, at the time they were drawn, the space existed only in the mind of the designer.

# Furniture in Plans

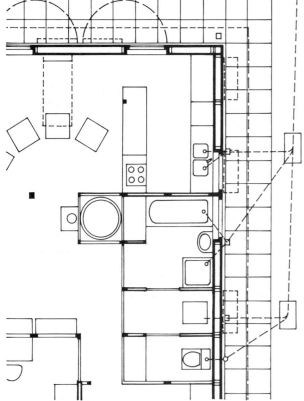

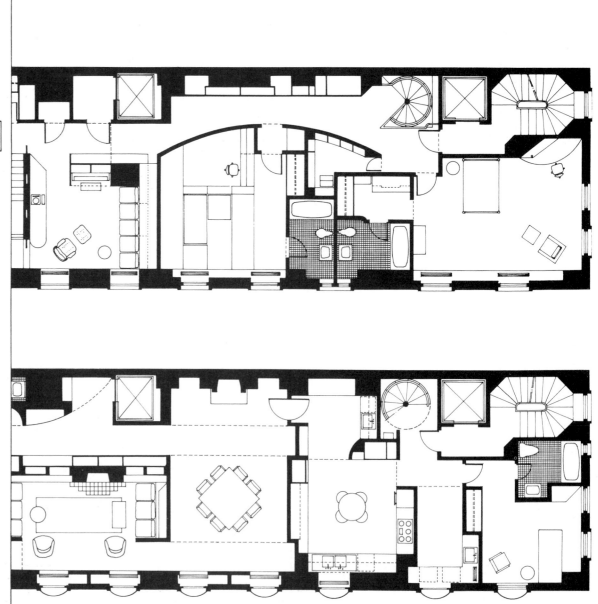

Fixed furniture and fittings should always be included in a plan, especially those in kitchens and bathrooms that are connected to water and waste services. These are described from an aerial view using a minimal, representative outline. Ready-cut stencils and pressure transfer versions are available at the different scales for their rapid installation in drawings, but many architects tend to devise and stick to their own personal symbols.

Loose furniture can also be included in plans and can be shown clearly with a minimum of fuss. This is considered "good practice" by many designers since the positioning of seating, tables, cupboards, and, especially, beds is seen, in itself, as a design exercise that tests the viability of the spaces they are meant to occupy.

# Furniture in Elevations

plan

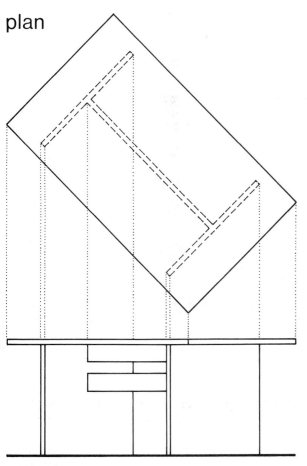

elevation

The presence of tables, chairs, beds, and other furniture will provide character to interior elevation drawings and will also help to communicate the function of the space. Usually drawn in side or front profile, the forms of furniture can also be vertically rotated to present the viewer with a three-quarter view of two of its sides. However, as elevation flattens all the layers of information in its field of view into a single vertical plane—regardless of their position in space—all forms that are parallel to its line of view keep their true-scale dimensions.

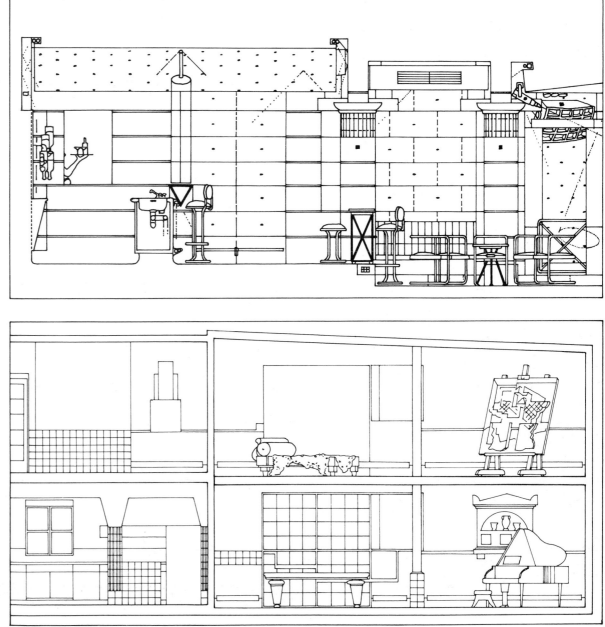

# Furniture in Axonometrics

These two cutaway plan projection drawings demonstrate the scale-giving effect furniture provides to axonometric interior spaces. This effect is particularly marked in the drawing below--taken from one by Mark Lintott--of a design for a small apartment for a pop-star client. Here, the cubic hardness of the interior is offset by the use of drapes and loose fabric covers on furniture--an intervention that brings a freehand line quality to the potential bleakness of the ruled line.

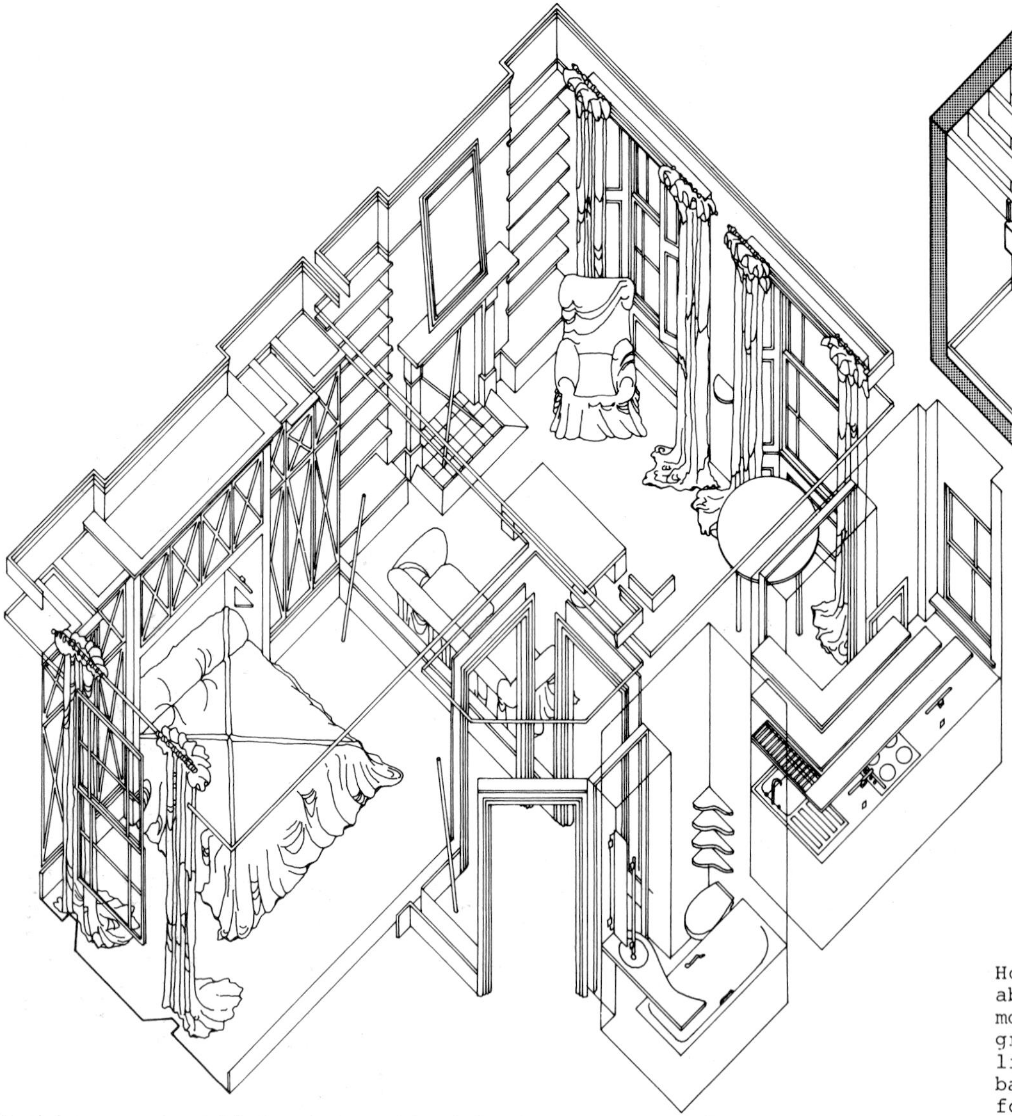

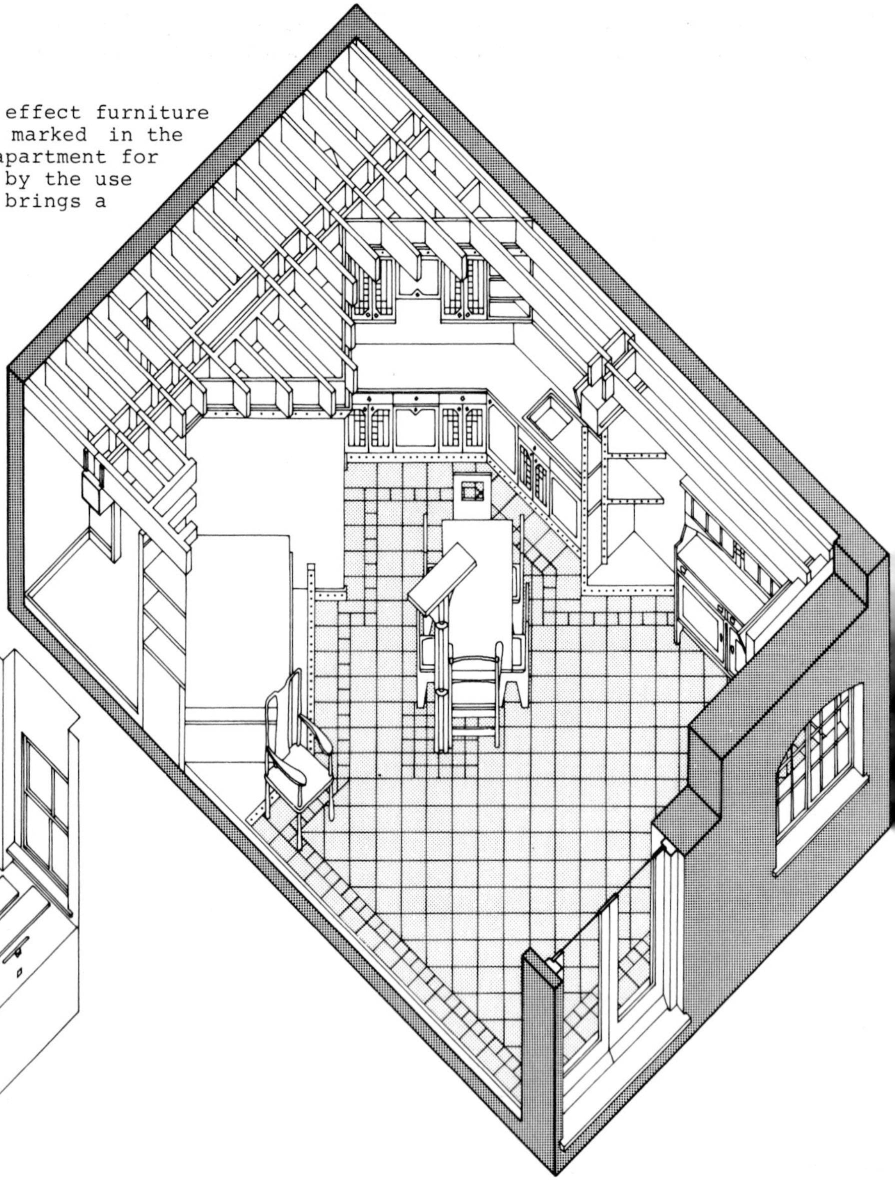

However, the rectangularity of the kitchen-dining area shown above includes a diagonal interplay that is reflected in the modules of its floorscape and along which the central furniture group is aligned. In this drawing, deviation from the straight line is represented by the curved profiles of the arms and backrest of the left-hand chair. A basic construction pattern for the furniture in both drawings is shown on the facing page.

# Furniture in Axonometrics

This sequence of drawing stages shows the basic evolution of subtle deviations from the cubic nature of the axonometric projection of furniture depicted in the drawings on the facing page. In each case, a simple framework of ruled guidelines drawn lightly in graphite paves the way for an informed and freehand ink line. Notice that the edges of nearer horizontal planes of the bed (a) have been omitted from the final delineation. Instead, these have been suggested by the ends of the lines of vertical folds. Also notice that--as always in axonometrics--the curvilinear shapes of the chair arms (e) have been found within the two rectangular "boxes" provided by the preparatory underdrawing.

# Classic Chairs

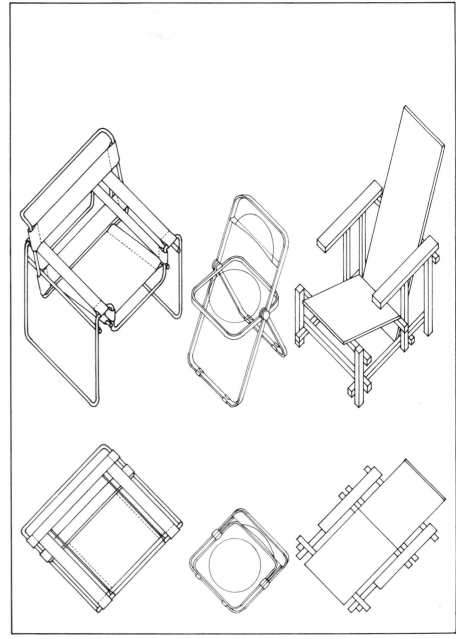

The majority of so-called classic chairs are designed by architects, not furniture designers. Furthermore, these chairs seem to function as a microcosm of each architect's design philosophy. Typical of this kind of embodiment is the Red and Blue Chair designed in 1917 by the Dutch de Stijl architect Gerrit Rietveld. Such chairs are often introduced to interior elevations and projection drawings to add a touch of class. Therefore, we first present a range of elevational silhouettes, based on a guide produced by Terry Trickett, followed by a selection of chairs shown in plan and axonometric projections.

Reading from left to right, the following chairs are shown in elevation: Roquebrune; Plia chair; PEL RP7 nesting chair; Breuer's Cesca; Jacobsen 3100 three-legged chair; Jacobsen Swan chair; Robin Day's polypropylene chair; Mies's Brno; Eames GRP dining chair; Mies's MR dining chair; Aalto Viipuri stool; Aalto Paimio armchair; Hans Coray's Landi chair; Mies's Barcelona chair; Stam chair; Thonet armchair; Le Corbusier's chaise longue; Rietveld Red and Blue chair; Le Corbusier's Basculant; Eames lounge chair; Eames aluminum chair; Le Corbusier's Grand Confort; Thonet dining chair.

# Furniture in Perspectives

Rather than invent furniture, draw from elegant examples. Then, having done so, avoid rendering them exclusively in tone at the expense of the spaces they occupy. As with all contextual information, this strategy will distract from and obscure the architectural focus of your perspective drawing. Here, we exemplify four examples of interior perspectives in which the inclusion of furniture coexists happily within the overall technique used for each drawing. This sequence begins with a detail taken from the work of master draftsman Romaldo Giurgola (above), whose selective but distinctive line and value technique is not used to highlight objects in space but to "sculpt" the interior space itself. Notice, too, that Giurgola's drawing also incorporates figures in close proximity to the furniture to underline the sense of scale.

# Staircases in Sections and Elevations

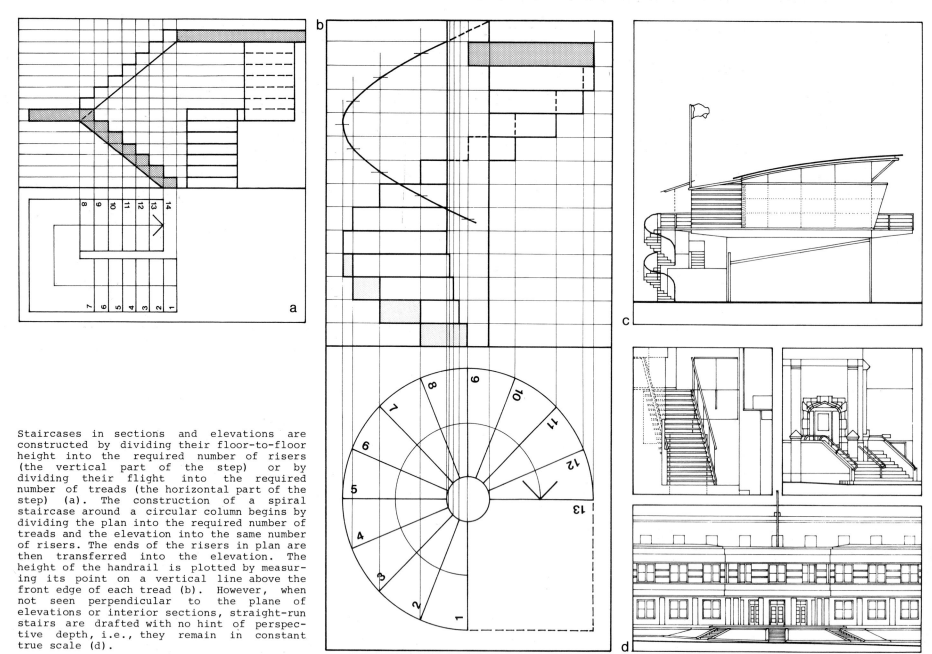

Staircases in sections and elevations are constructed by dividing their floor-to-floor height into the required number of risers (the vertical part of the step) or by dividing their flight into the required number of treads (the horizontal part of the step) (a). The construction of a spiral staircase around a circular column begins by dividing the plan into the required number of treads and the elevation into the same number of risers. The ends of the risers in plan are then transferred into the elevation. The height of the handrail is plotted by measuring its point on a vertical line above the front edge of each tread (b). However, when not seen perpendicular to the plane of elevations or interior sections, straight-run stairs are drafted with no hint of perspective depth, i.e., they remain in constant true scale (d).

# Staircases in Axonometrics

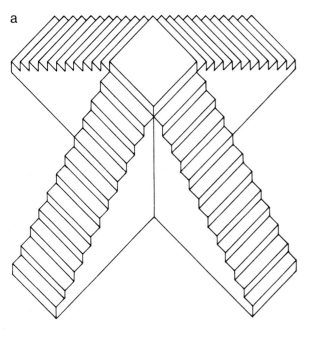

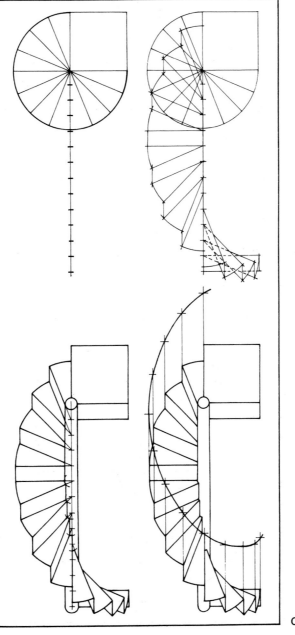

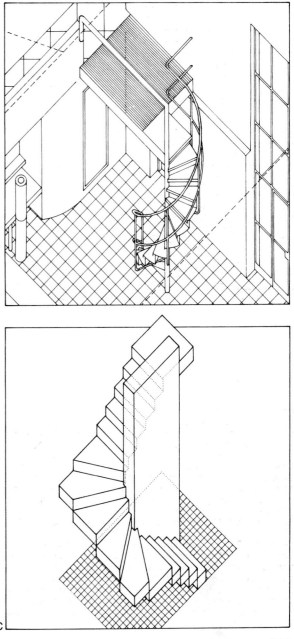

The construction of straight-run and U-type stairs begins by "ghosting" their plan and floor-to-landing height. The positions of treads and risers are plotted up from the plan in true scale (a). Spiral staircases in axonometrics begin with the upper floor plan containing the required number of treads. After projecting the support column and using this as a scale for the risers, the position of each step can be plotted in the vertical plane of the spiral. The step transfer process from plan to axonometric is the equivalent of sliding a tracing of the plan incrementally down the riser scale and marking off each tread in its location on the spiral (b). Here are two examples of staircases--a spiral and a winder--found in axonometrics (c).

# Spiral Staircases in Perspectives

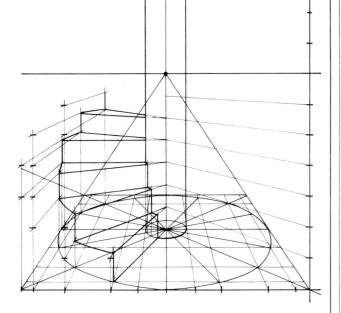

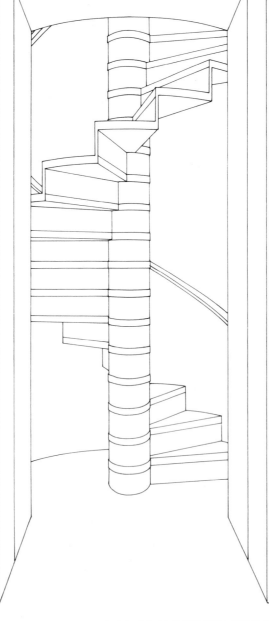

Spiral staircases are constructed using perspective coordinates through plan projection --the treads' and risers' true dimensions first being measured on the picture plane before being projected onto the equivalently marked central column. However, since the projection process can be time-consuming, and since badly drawn freehand versions can often ruin a perspective drawing, many architects use a shortcut by adapting spiral staircases from photographs. The drawings shown on this page were done using this method--the photograph first being photocopied, then resized prior to tracing directly into the drawing.

# Staircases in Perspectives

# Fluttering Entourage

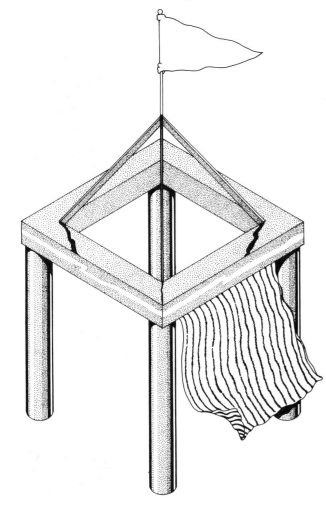

Aside from the insertion of figures and trees to establish scale and context, another common means of importing these qualities-- together with an added dimension of movement --is the draping of facades with curtains and the hoisting of flags to celebrate the pinnacles of high buildings and to frame major public entrances. Easily drawn in freehand using a continuous or broken line, these elements create a lively contrast to hardline design drawings as well as indicate visual evidence of air movement around and through the space of design proposals.

**74**

# Sculptural Entourage

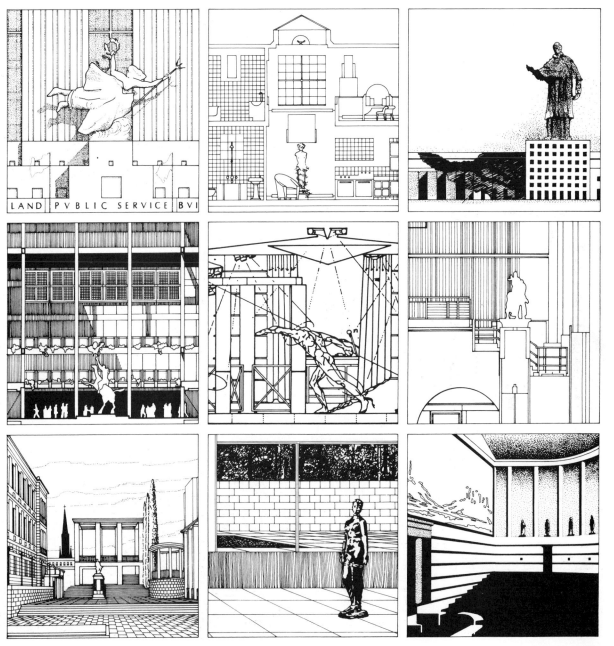

An aspect of design drawings that is often trivialized is the depiction of sculpture, particularly modern sculpture. This trivialization can also extend to urban focal events, such as fountains and monuments that, being drawn in a throwaway fashion, tend to appear as urban design caricatures. This graphic attitude is sad because, if backed by reference to existing precedents and a little care in their delineation, these environmental points of interest can be included in drawings in a convincing manner. For example, this page is devoted to such nodes found in a wide range of architects' graphics. In occupying an important part of the parent drawing, the environmental object has, in each case, been drafted with care and attention.

# Elevational Features

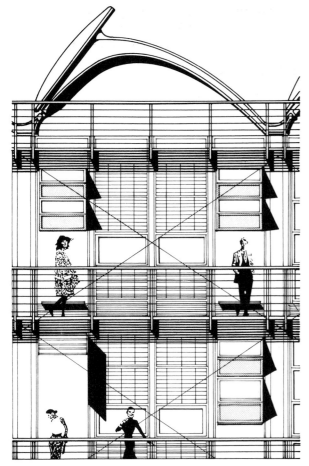

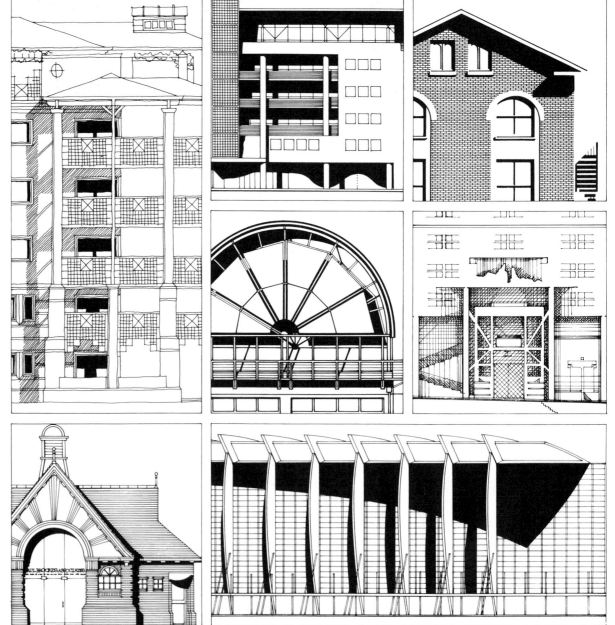

Architectural features that articulate skyline silhouette or indent, or project from
the face of buildings, tend to give a building visual interest and individuality. Therefore, their presence--especially in eleva-
tions--needs to be carefully drawn and, in
some cases, slightly overstated. To avoid
having such features lost or misread, it is a
good idea to focus on their delineation and,
whenever possible, render their presence
three-dimensional with the use of shade and
shadow. It is the graphic depiction of
materials together with shade and shadow
construction and rendering that takes us into
the next chapter.

# 4 SURFACE, SHADE, AND SHADOW

# Building Materials in Elevation

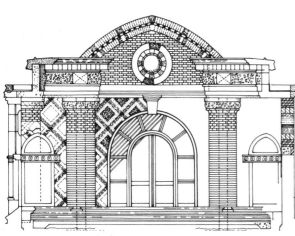

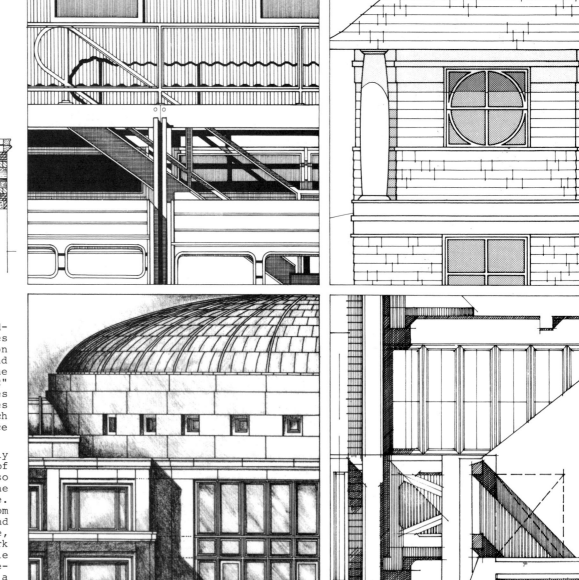

Generally speaking, the materials of a building shown in elevation are expressed in lines that describe the patterns of connection between the assembly of modular units and decorative or structural components. In the larger scale elevation drawings, such as 1/2" = 1' (1:20) and 1/4" = 1' (1:50), these lines are liable to account for all visible edges and joints and, thereby, can produce a rich expression of structural pattern and surface grain.

This searching attitude to detailing not only reflects an awareness of how the elements of a building will be assembled, it also portrays a more honest impression of the appearance of the resulting architecture. In addition, this attitude takes us away from blandness and involves us in the physical and tactile aspects of built form. For example, in the elevation above, taken from the work of John Outram, we can sense the tactile quality of this design proposal. His line-work transcends abstraction to describe a sequence of surfaces rich in pattern and textural diversity.

# Rendering Techniques for Materials in Elevation

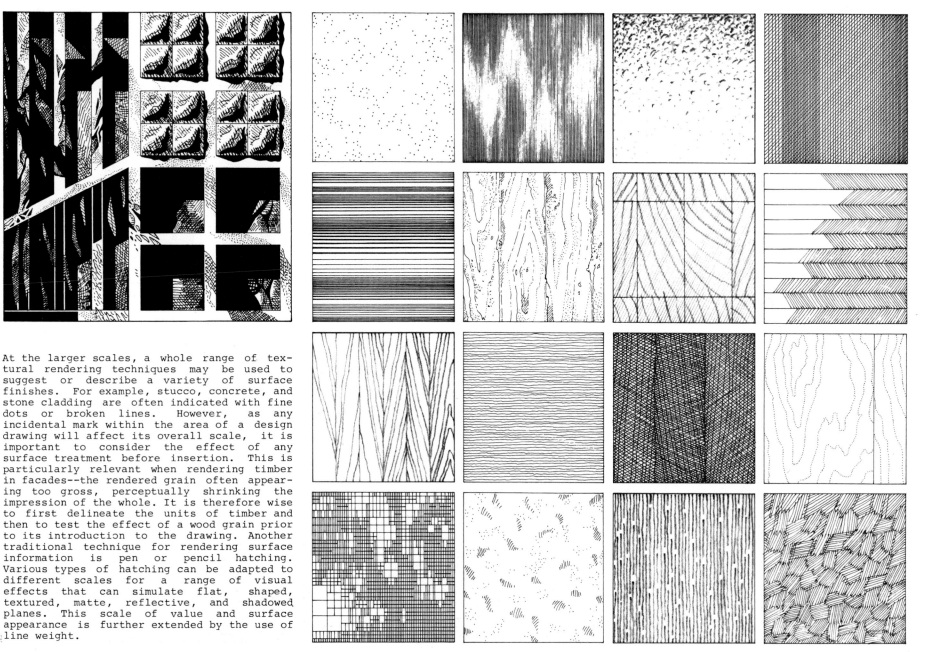

At the larger scales, a whole range of textural rendering techniques may be used to suggest or describe a variety of surface finishes. For example, stucco, concrete, and stone cladding are often indicated with fine dots or broken lines. However, as any incidental mark within the area of a design drawing will affect its overall scale, it is important to consider the effect of any surface treatment before insertion. This is particularly relevant when rendering timber in facades--the rendered grain often appearing too gross, perceptually shrinking the impression of the whole. It is therefore wise to first delineate the units of timber and then to test the effect of a wood grain prior to its introduction to the drawing. Another traditional technique for rendering surface information is pen or pencil hatching. Various types of hatching can be adapted to different scales for a range of visual effects that can simulate flat, shaped, textured, matte, reflective, and shadowed planes. This scale of value and surface appearance is further extended by the use of line weight.

# Brickwork

## Brick Bonds

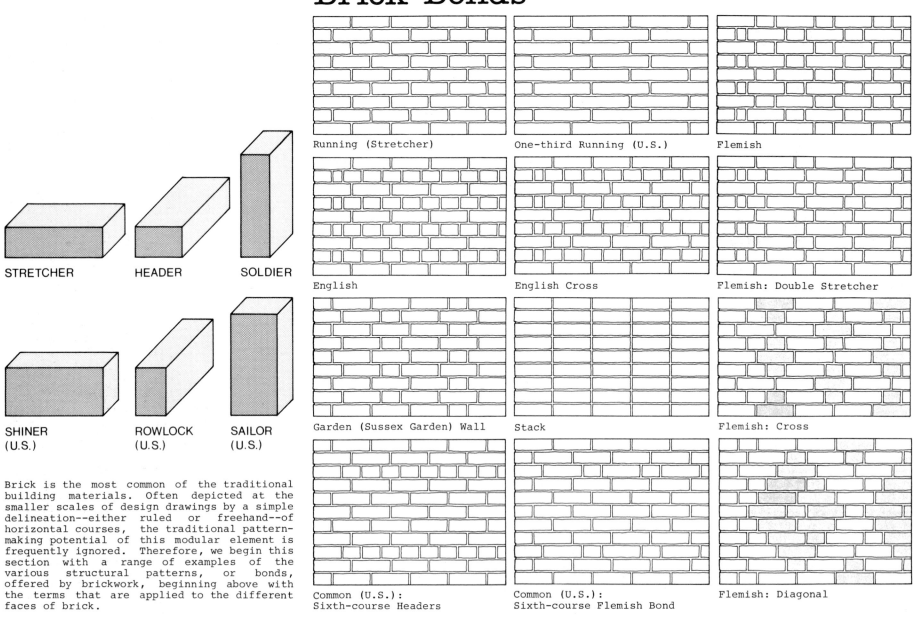

STRETCHER    HEADER    SOLDIER

SHINER (U.S.)    ROWLOCK (U.S.)    SAILOR (U.S.)

Running (Stretcher)    One-third Running (U.S.)    Flemish

English    English Cross    Flemish: Double Stretcher

Garden (Sussex Garden) Wall    Stack    Flemish: Cross

Common (U.S.): Sixth-course Headers    Common (U.S.): Sixth-course Flemish Bond    Flemish: Diagonal

Brick is the most common of the traditional building materials. Often depicted at the smaller scales of design drawings by a simple delineation--either ruled or freehand--of horizontal courses, the traditional pattern-making potential of this modular element is frequently ignored. Therefore, we begin this section with a range of examples of the various structural patterns, or bonds, offered by brickwork, beginning above with the terms that are applied to the different faces of brick.

# Brickwork and Blockwork

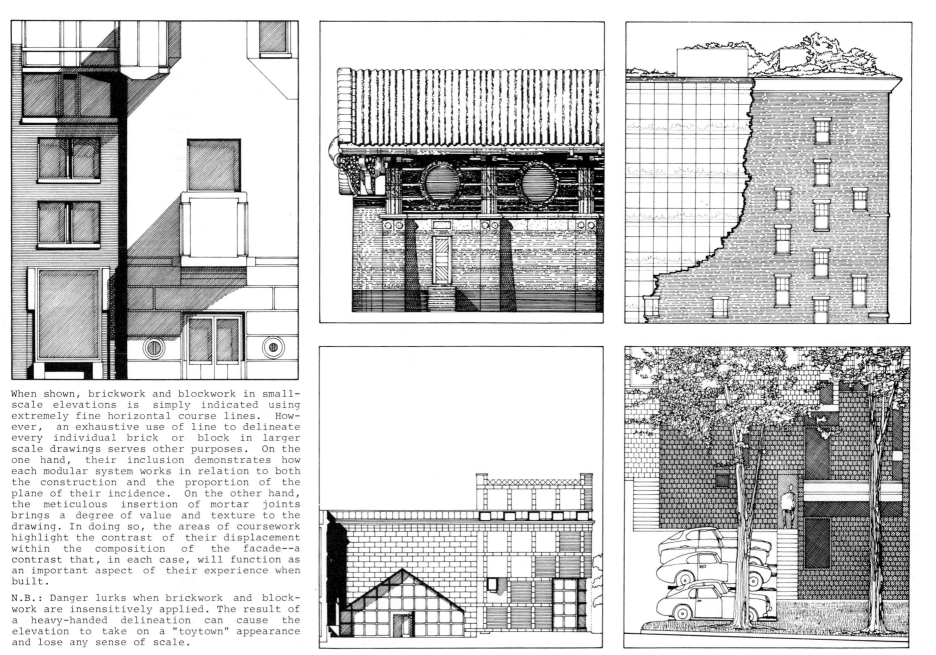

When shown, brickwork and blockwork in small-scale elevations is simply indicated using extremely fine horizontal course lines. However, an exhaustive use of line to delineate every individual brick or block in larger scale drawings serves other purposes. On the one hand, their inclusion demonstrates how each modular system works in relation to both the construction and the proportion of the plane of their incidence. On the other hand, the meticulous insertion of mortar joints brings a degree of value and texture to the drawing. In doing so, the areas of coursework highlight the contrast of their displacement within the composition of the facade—a contrast that, in each case, will function as an important aspect of their experience when built.

N.B.: Danger lurks when brickwork and blockwork are insensitively applied. The result of a heavy-handed delineation can cause the elevation to take on a "toytown" appearance and lose any sense of scale.

# Stone Facings and Coursework

Masonry and its various methods of construction offers a rich variety of surface pattern and texture for the vertical planes of building designs. Therefore, when employing stone, architects will tend to indicate its effect meticulously at the larger scales and draw the detail of its coursework with a certain degree of care and attention. However, to avoid a "stone wallpaper" effect in dressed stone facades, a good technique is to allow the mortar joints to "erode" in response to the effect of light arriving from the conventional direction in elevations, i.e., diagonally from upper left. This technique emphasizes the junctions of lines and the underedges of courses (the shadow-casting lines). Meanwhile, those edges receiving light use finer lines and are allowed to occasionally break. The illustration on the right shows a progressive scale of decomposition using a freehand ink line above a penciled guideline.

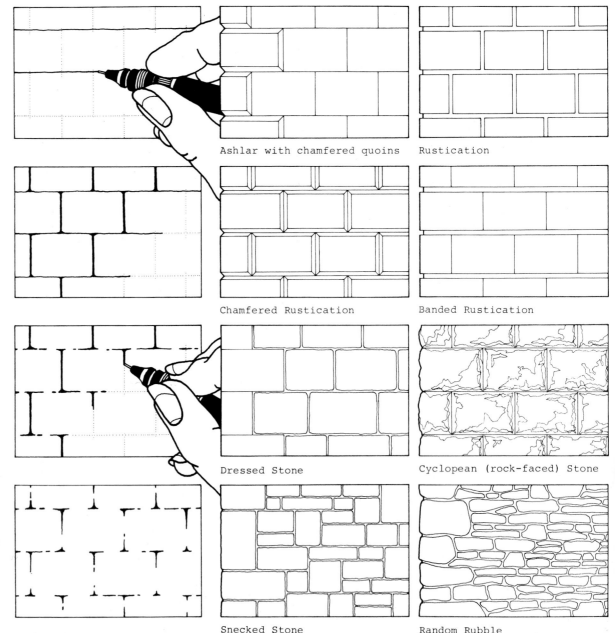

Ashlar with chamfered quoins

Rustication

Chamfered Rustication

Banded Rustication

Dressed Stone

Cyclopean (rock-faced) Stone

Snecked Stone

Random Rubble

# Masonry in Design Drawings

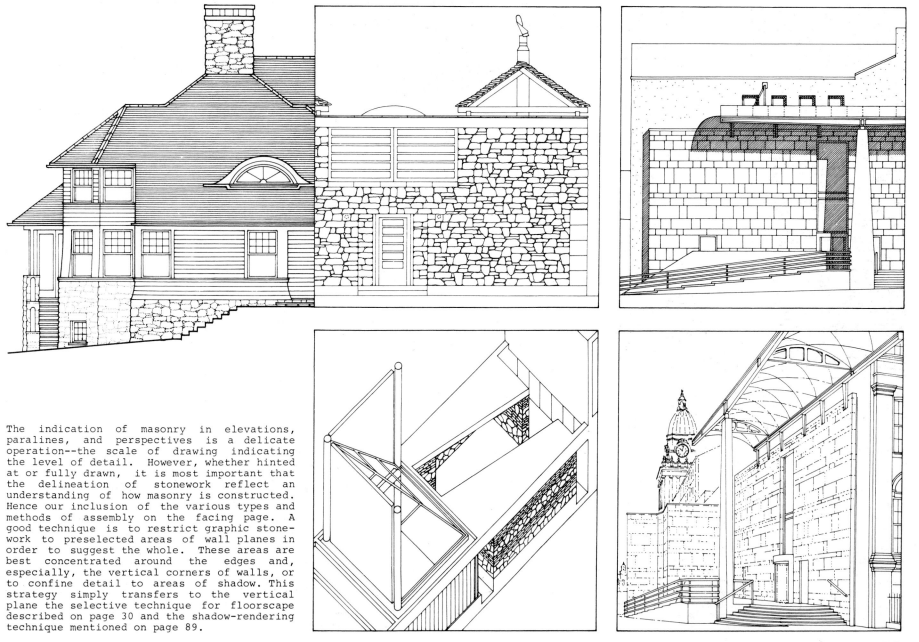

The indication of masonry in elevations, paralines, and perspectives is a delicate operation--the scale of drawing indicating the level of detail. However, whether hinted at or fully drawn, it is most important that the delineation of stonework reflect an understanding of how masonry is constructed. Hence our inclusion of the various types and methods of assembly on the facing page. A good technique is to restrict graphic stone-work to preselected areas of wall planes in order to suggest the whole. These areas are best concentrated around the edges and, especially, the vertical corners of walls, or to confine detail to areas of shadow. This strategy simply transfers to the vertical plane the selective technique for floorscape described on page 30 and the shadow-rendering technique mentioned on page 89.

# Marble

Being an exotic material, the subtle surface of marble is used by many architects--either in its true crystalline limestone form or as a trompe l'oeil, sham, and decoratively painted application to the planes of interiors. Whether real or an illusion, its rendition in design drawings demands a fresh and nervous freehand line to suggest the subtlety of its streaked surface grain--a pattern that is also used descriptively in its conventional symbol for working drawings (see pages 24-25). A good strategy for representing this pattern without disturbing the integrity of a pen-drawn design graphic is to delineate the grain in pencil. Otherwise, an ink rendition--as exploited in some of the examples shown here--will register as the compositional center of attention. In any case, before working directly on a presentation drawing, it is always wise to first make a series of practice runs.

# Suggesting Concrete and Timber

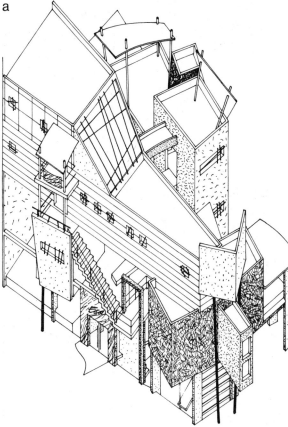

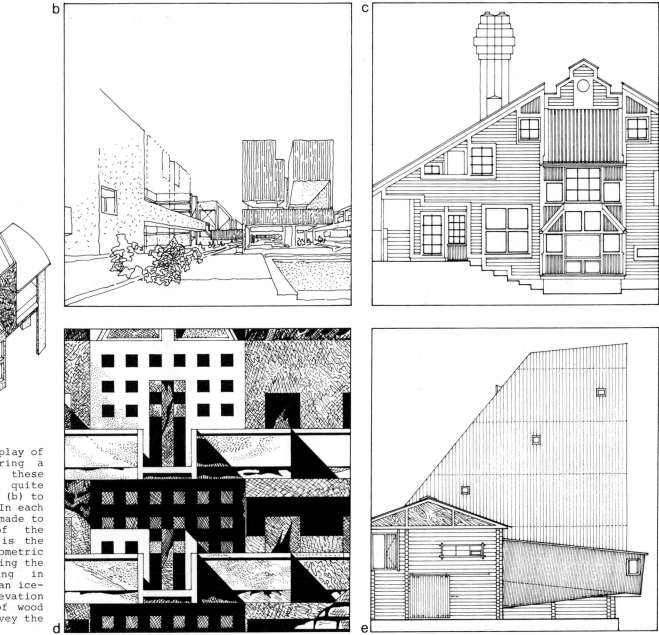

Even when minimally rendered, an interplay of suggested material finishes can bring a textural richness to a drawing. As these demonstrate, the suggestion can be quite sparse and range from the sketchlike (b) to the more formal and calculated (c). In each case, however, an attempt has been made to communicate the tactile quality of the architectural form. Most interesting is the use of textural technique on the axonometric (a) that is a student design exploiting the tactile impression of his building in response to the project—a design for an ice-cream and fur shop. Meanwhile, the elevation of a timber building (e) uses a hint of wood grain and an almost rustic line to convey the quality of a log cabin.

# Techniques for Glass

Four techniques for simulating glazing in larger scale elevations include: (a) A layer of medium tone wash with, if required, a highlight inserted by scraping the freshly applied liquid with the corner of a credit card (when dry, a darker wash is overlaid to express the shadow); (b) A graphite version of this technique ends when the highlight is quickly inserted with the flick of an eraser; (c) A diagonal ink-line hatching can receive a secondary hatching to indicate the shadow before the highlight is deftly scratched away with the corner of a razor blade; (d) An alternative ink-line technique may or may not use broken lines to suggest the reflective quality of glass --a thicker version of the same line being confined to the shadow area.

Being a reflective material, glass in elevations can often pose a graphic problem. Traditionally, elevations have tended to either leave windows blank or have them subjected to a dark, even ink wash. The latter technique was particularly popular with neo-Palladian draftsmen, but the flatness of their washes tended to make fenestration appear dull and lacking in sparkle. Therefore, when not using a blue or blue-gray marker or watercolor wash, areas of glass offer the potential of a series of techniques that, with a careful use of highlights, recognize both the reflective quality of the material and the fact that windows often present the darkest element in a facade.

# Techniques for Glass

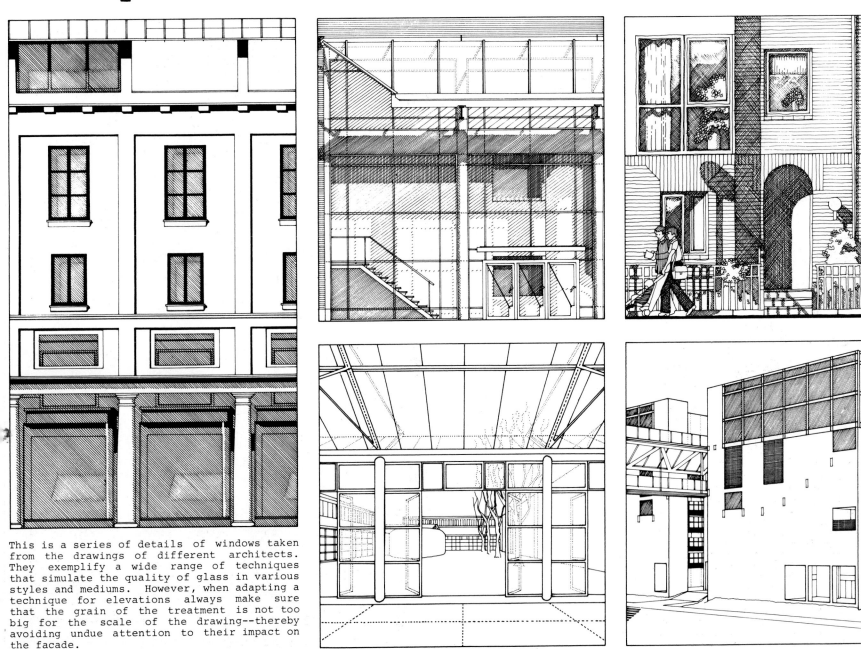

This is a series of details of windows taken from the drawings of different architects. They exemplify a wide range of techniques that simulate the quality of glass in various styles and mediums. However, when adapting a technique for elevations always make sure that the grain of the treatment is not too big for the scale of the drawing--thereby avoiding undue attention to their impact on the facade.

# Mirror Glass Techniques

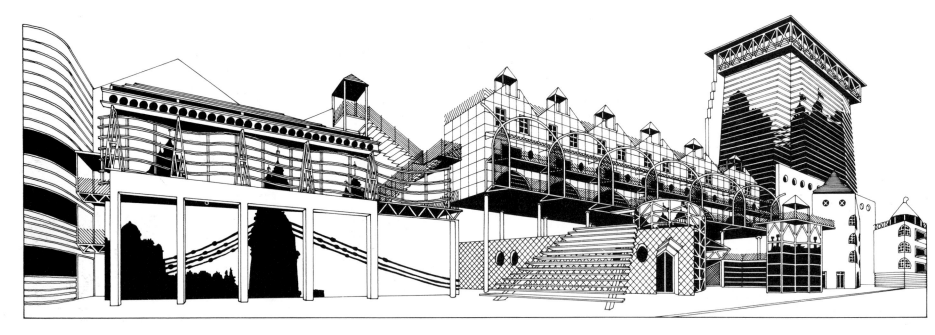

Larger areas of glazing, such as curtain walling, can be rendered to appear as reflecting the elevations of planes that are immediately adjacent to it. On faceted-glass facades, reflections can be distorted or shown as an undisturbed mirror image. In either event, this technique relies upon the compartmentalization of mullions to remind the viewer that the image is a reflection. When it doesn't, the technique fails. Techniques range from the rendering of halftone reflections to the sharp contrast between white and a solid black silhouette.

# Shadow-Rendering Techniques

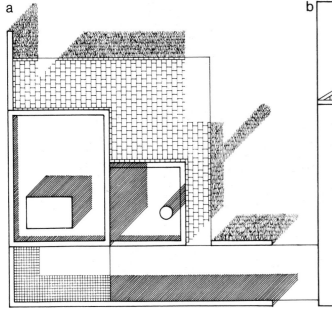

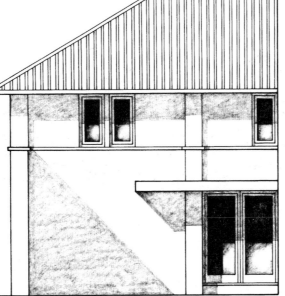

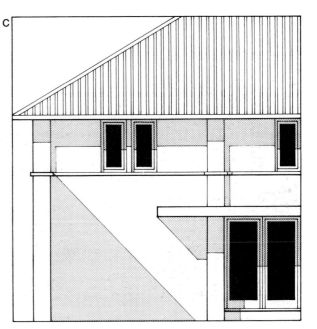

The function of shadow rendering in design drawings is to indicate the height of mass above the ground plane or the depth of projecting mass in the vertical plane and, through value contrast, to elaborate the three-dimensional quality of a building form. In elevations and site plans, however, the rendering technique can both indicate changes in surface and topography and--at the larger scales--hint at surface texture (a). The traditional method of rendering shadows is a flat, transparent ink or graphite wash that allows all the lines within it to remain visually intact (b). Today, these washes have been almost completely replaced by the instant tones provided by dry-transfer screens (c). Another common method is the use of vertical or 45-degree fine-line hatching-- the latter following the direction of the shadow (d). A selective but successful technique for depicting both shadow and the nature of a surface is to confine the rendering exclusively to the areas of shadow and, at the same time, expose the joints between modular materials (e).

# Cylinders in Elevation

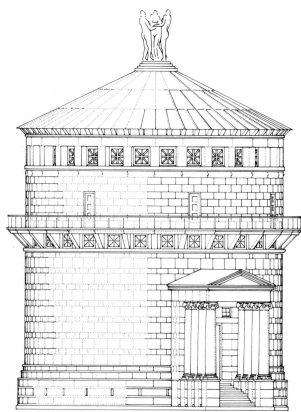

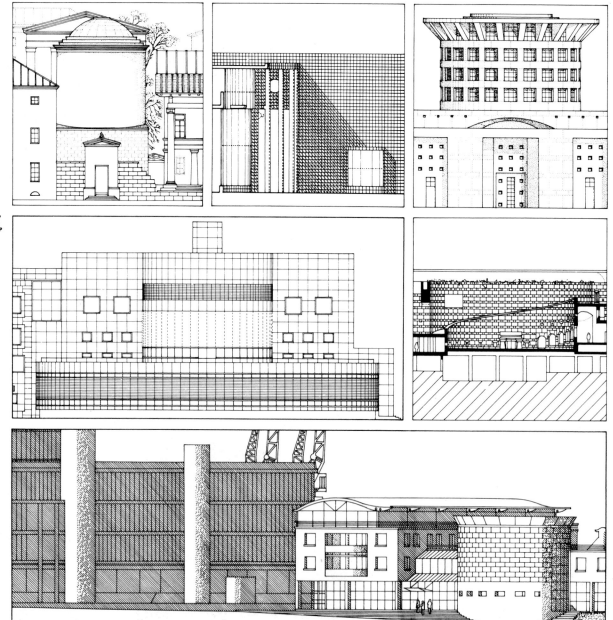

When towers, bays, the envelopes of spiral staircases, and circular buildings appear in elevations, they present a comparatively easy rendering task. When drafted at small scale, the main technique is to use horizontal or vertical shading that is encouraged to fade consistently as it moves into the light. Alternative techniques include the delineation of mortar joints—the vertical joints implying the roundness—and the confinement of modular joints to the area of shade. Larger scale drawings provide the opportunity for the vertical banding of a value progression from deep shade to light. This degree of tonal modeling also allows the added bonus of indulging in the effect of reflected light (see page 91).

# Reflected Light Techniques

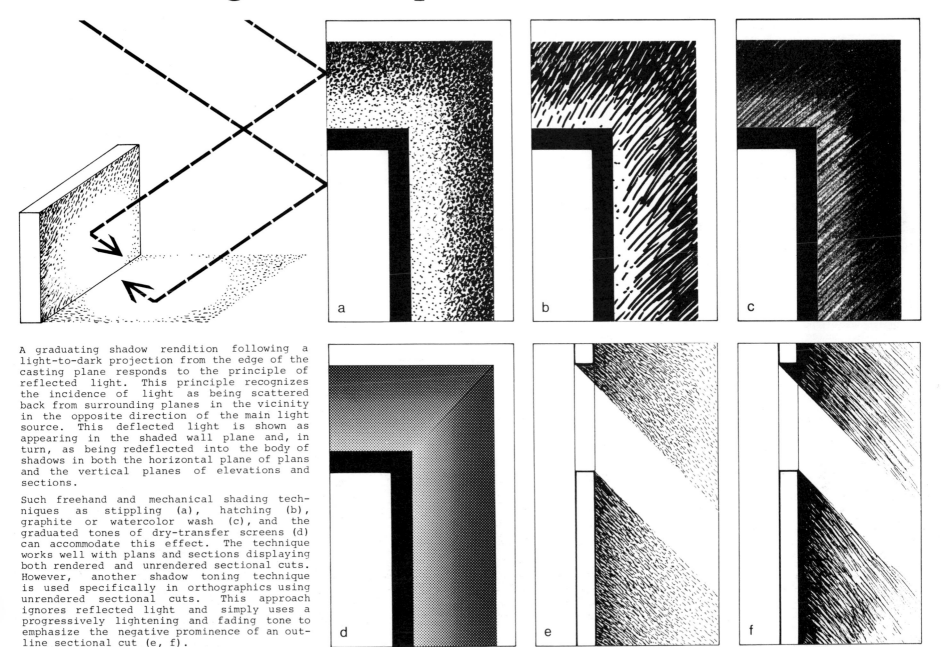

A graduating shadow rendition following a light-to-dark projection from the edge of the casting plane responds to the principle of reflected light. This principle recognizes the incidence of light as being scattered back from surrounding planes in the vicinity in the opposite direction of the main light source. This deflected light is shown as appearing in the shaded wall plane and, in turn, as being redeflected into the body of shadows in both the horizontal plane of plans and the vertical planes of elevations and sections.

Such freehand and mechanical shading techniques as stippling (a), hatching (b), graphite or watercolor wash (c), and the graduated tones of dry-transfer screens (d) can accommodate this effect. The technique works well with plans and sections displaying both rendered and unrendered sectional cuts. However, another shadow toning technique is used specifically in orthographics using unrendered sectional cuts. This approach ignores reflected light and simply uses a progressively lightening and fading tone to emphasize the negative prominence of an outline sectional cut (e, f).

# Shade and Shadow: Basic Geometric Solids

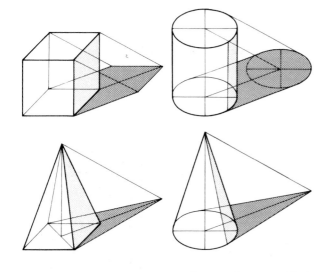

As architecture comprises form and space that is usually generated by basic geometric solids, the construction of shade and shadow to intensify its three-dimensional illusion in design drawings is not as difficult as it might seem. Shade represents the unlit areas of the surface of an illuminated object, whereas shadows are projected onto another surface from an object that receives light (above).

To plot the shadow cast by a square figure standing forward of an elevation plane, reference is made to a plan. Shadow construction is plotted after projecting 45-degree lines from the top corners of the elevation together with similar projections from the plan. Where the lines on the plan contact the vertical plane, perpendiculars are projected up to intersect the lines drawn on elevation (a). Using the plan projection principle, shade and shadows on cylindrical (b) and conical figures (c) can be quickly constructed. Shadow construction for a sphere begins with 45-degree lines in the conventional angle of light on the elevation. These give both the points from which its shade is found and, when transferred to the plan, provide the framework from which the elliptical shape of its shadow is plotted (d).

N.B.: Notice that the direction of light in both plan and elevation follows the convention for shadows (see page 28).

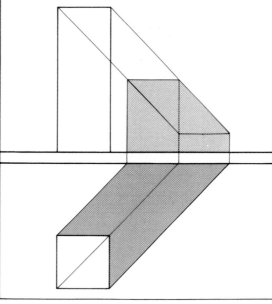

a

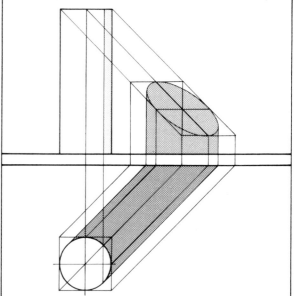

b

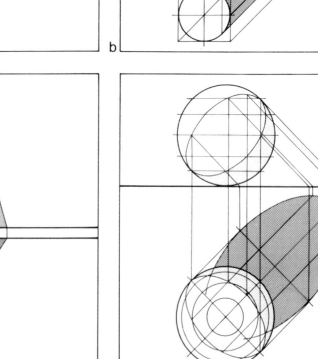

c

d

# Shade and Shadow: Angular Projections

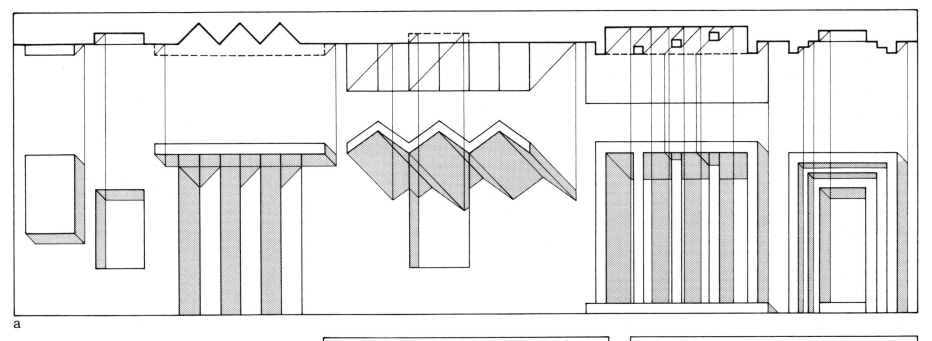

a

Using the plan projection method, a whole range of shadows cast by recesses, projections, and objects forward of the elevation can be quickly plotted. The effect of the 45-degree shadow convention appears convincing as it corresponds to average daylight conditions. Also, as the dimensions of shadows are generally the same as the objects from which they are cast, construction is fast using a T-square and triangle (a).

The plotting method for shadows cast from a chimney onto a pitched roof transfers points from an auxiliary side elevation rather than a plan. The point at which the top of the stack strikes the inclined plane in side elevation is transferred onto the front elevation (b).

Similarly, to plot a shadow from a dormer window, points are first projected on a side elevation back at 45 degrees onto the inclined plane. These points are then transferred horizontally to the front elevation before being projected along the 45-degree bearing of the shape of the shadow on the pitched roof (c).

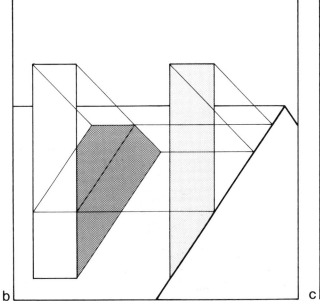

b

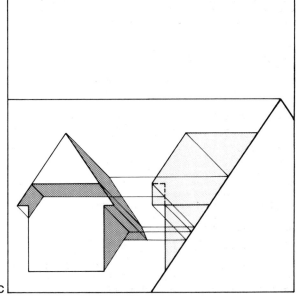

c

# Shade and Shadow: Stepped Forms

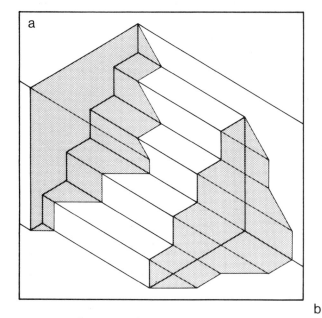

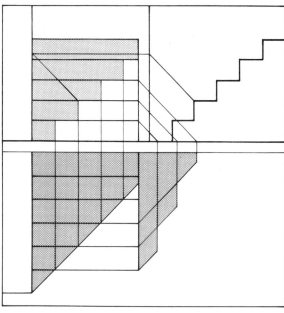

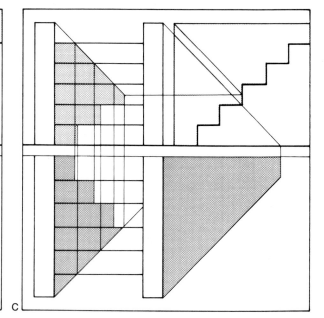

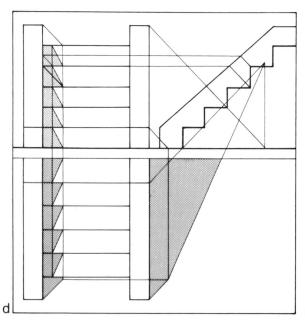

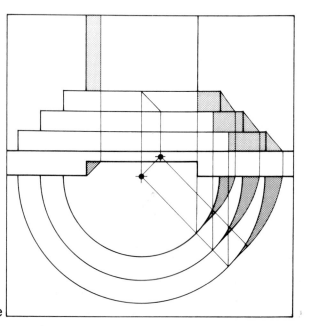

More complicated forms, such as flights of steps, might be seen to present a problem. But it should be remembered that a straight line seen perpendicular to the plane of an elevation appears as a point, and that shadows cast by this line in front elevation is always a 45-degree line--whatever the form of the surface receiving its shadow (a). Here we illustrate a few common types of steps with their shadow-casting walls parallel to the slope of their flight, plus one example involving circular steps.

Vertical shade lines (represented by the left-hand side walls) cast a plane of shadow back and away from the viewer and to the right at 45 degrees in elevation. The side elevation shows the distance to the right from the vertical shade line that causes the shadow. Using the point transfer method, the shadow of any straight line can be plotted by finding the shadows of the ends of that in the side elevation (b, c, and d).

The shadows cast by a circle will appear as the same size as the circle casting the shadow. The position of the shadow is found by slipping the center of the circle back along a 45-degree line to a length corresponding to the height of the step (e).

# Shade and Shadow: Curved and Circular Projections

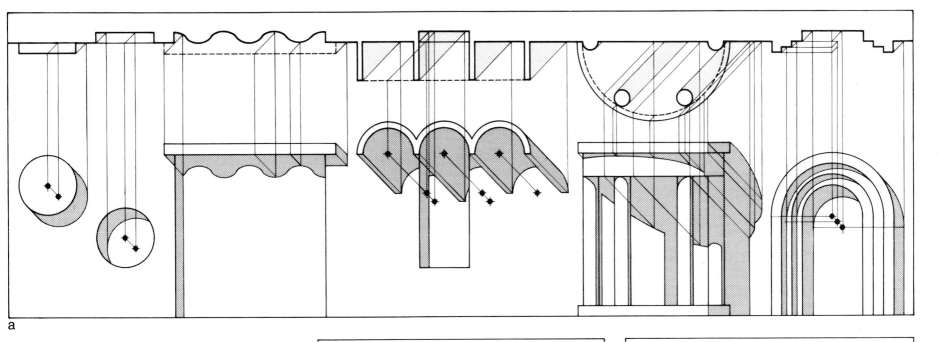

a

Most of the shadows cast by curved and circular recesses and projections can be resolved in elevation using the 45-degree plan projection method. Notice that the shadows cast from the projecting cylinder and cylindrical recess are plotted by slipping the center of the circle along the appropriate direction of the 45-degree angle to a length equal to their depth. The method for plotting the shadow from the semicircular canopy is the point transfer system, i.e., the projection of key points along its edge from plan to elevation. Meanwhile, the shadow of a vaulted canopy is simply a 45-degree projection of its depth as seen in elevation (a).

To cast a shadow from an arcade onto a back wall, first project the inner and outer faces of the semicircular arches in plan and elevation at points 1 and 3 together with the inner and outer points (2) at the arch's center (b). Where these projectors intersect finds the shadow's edge formed by the two faces of the arch. Continue plotting for further arches along the arcade (c).

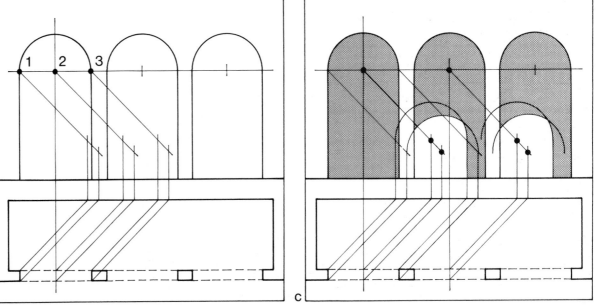

b

c

# Shade and Shadow: Cylinders

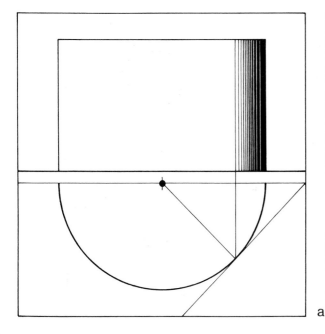

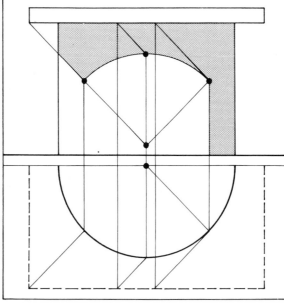

a

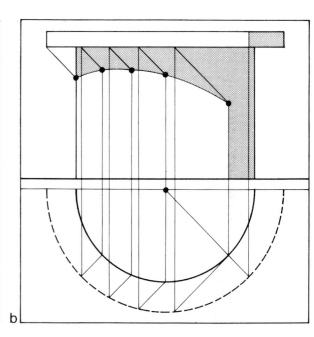

b

The shaded area of curved forms, such as the cylinder above, is found from its shadow line on plan. However, shade is rarely seen as a hard edge on cylinders and is usually rendered as fading from light to dark. The construction of the shadow from a square block above a cylinder begins by plotting the 45-degree shadow line from the corner of the block. The curved line of shadow is determined by transferring 45-degree projectors along key points between the cylinder and the edge of the block in plan until the curve of the shadow in elevation meets the vertical line of shade (a). The same point transfer method is used to plot the shadow of a curved cap above the cylinder (b). Meanwhile, the shadow cast from a block above a hollow cylinder is plotted from its shadow line in plan; the curved part of the shadow being drawn with a compass (c). The shadow area of a hollow cylinder (d) begins at point A; the curving part of the shadow being plotted uses the point transfer method.

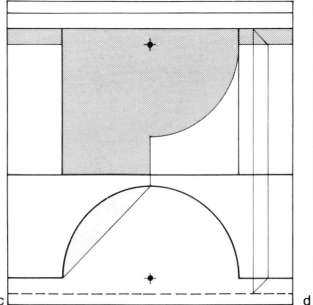

c

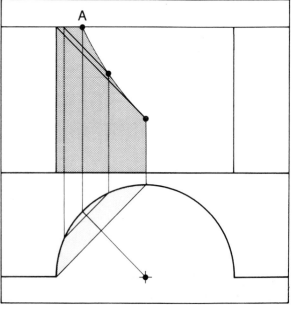

d

# Shade and Shadow: Hemispheres and Domes

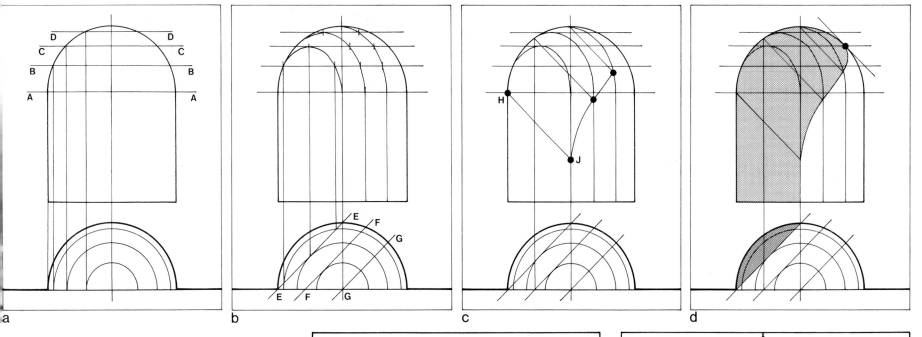

a

b

c

d

To determine the shadow on a niche, draw contours A, B, C, D through the spherical head in elevation and reproduce these contours in plan (a). Then draw the lines EE, FF, and GG at 45 degrees on plan and, with reference to the points where they cut the contours, trace these sections on the elevation (b). Next, a 45-degree line drawn from point H on the section AA finds the extent of the vertical portion of the shadow at J. Similar projections from the points at which the remaining sections cut the face of the niche finds their equivalent points along the curvature of the shadow line through the spherical head of the niche (c). Finally, a tangent through the top of the head of the niche determines the point where this shadow line meets the face of the niche and completes the area of shadow which is now ready for rendering (d). Meanwhile, the illustrations on the right demonstrate the use of shade and shadow respectively on a dome (e) and a sectioned dome or quarter-sphere (f).

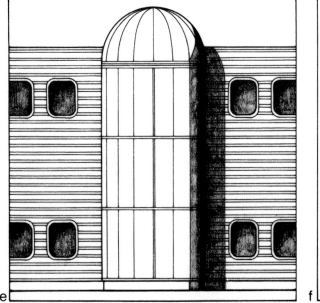

e

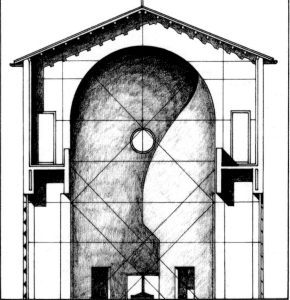

f

# Shade and Shadow: Axonometrics

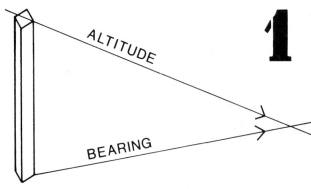

The length of shadow cast from an object is found at the intersection of the plan direction of light (bearing) and the angle, or altitude, of the sun's rays. Both of these components can be adjusted in axonometrics to suit the nature of the paraline information that is to be illuminated. However, one should always remember that when an object is sunlit, whatever the given or assumed bearing and angle, the rays of light appear as parallel lines.

**1**

The shadow cast from a box form is found by striking its shadow-casting points with light rays describing the angle of the altitude. The point at which this angle meets the bearing line (ground plane) provides the points from which the shadow is plotted.

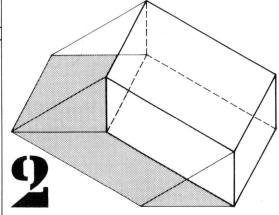

**2**

**3**

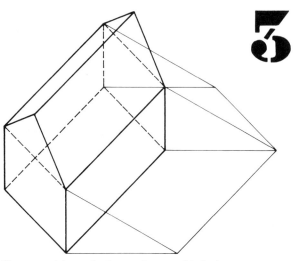

When casting shadows from slightly more complicated forms, project each element of that form separately. For example, for a basic gabled house form, first project the shadow of the "box" element.

**4**

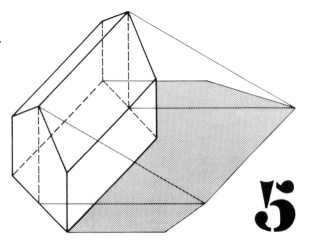

Then project the shadow of the gabled section as an extension of the shadow already established before completing its shape by connecting all the points.

Notice that the shadow points corresponding to each end of the ridge are found by bearing lines projected from points perpendicularly below them--the length of the shadow being found at their intersection with the corresponding angle of altitude.

**6**

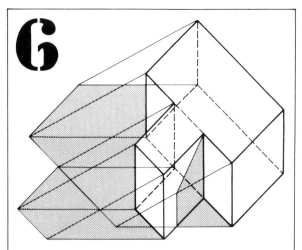

The same technique of separate shadow projection is used when one form projects from another, i.e., the shadow of each is projected independently to form the whole shape.

**5**

# 5 SKY, WATER, PLANES, BOATS, AND AUTOS

# Skies in Line

Linear sky techniques should be used essentially as a compositional device to counterpoint the shape of the elevation mass. For example, a suggestion of aerial delineation can bring a hint of depth and, if used diagonally, bring a useful fluidity to a static drawing. Also, the impression of taller buildings can be emphasized when seen against the horizontal stratification of simple cloud formations. Whatever their function, however, indications of cloudy skies should be used cautiously and employ finer lines so as not to detract from the architectural message.

# Skies in Tone

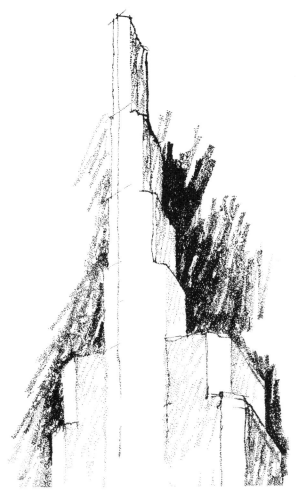

Tonal skies are usually used only when the architectural form is also heavily detailed in value, or when a dark backdrop is required to bring contrast to the skyline of an elevation. Generally speaking, the displacement of value in skies is employed to counterpoint the tone of the rendered building--dark areas of sky emphasizing light portions of an elevation and vice versa. This use of sky rendering as a compositional device is at its most basic when a diagonal arrangement of shape or application of tone counterpoints a horizontal-vertical building mass.

# Photocopied Sky

Occasionally, designers will add a photocopied sky tone directly to their elevations and perspectives in order to save time. These are culled from magazine photographs or sometimes from engravings such as those by Piranese. Once selected, the print or photograph is then enlarged or reduced on a photocopier to a size that will fit the drawing.

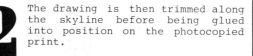

**1 2** The drawing is then trimmed along the skyline before being glued into position on the photocopied print.

**4** The two images can then be reproduced together on a photocopier to produce a new and second-stage original.

**3** To complete the integration between drawing and print, elements within the drawing are encouraged to overlap and enter the area of the printed sky mass.

This rapid sketch by Ian Ritchie is given a sense of drama using the photocopied sky technique. Notice how the photocopied sky has been introduced in two sections--with little concern for the resulting join.

# Airbrush and Spray Wash Skies

Here is an overcast and dark sky produced by the slickness of an air-brush or airpen, together with one using the more primitive method of stippling by blowing ink through a tube. In each case, a decision has been made to dramatize the elevation or perspective using high contrast--both within the sky area and between its backdrop and the building form. Used more for eye-catching competition submissions and drawings destined for half-tone publication, this technique works well for tall buildings--particularly when a glass tower mirrors the clouds. Otherwise, in order to maintain clarity, a stark contrast with a light-toned facade has to be employed.

# Spray Sky Techniques

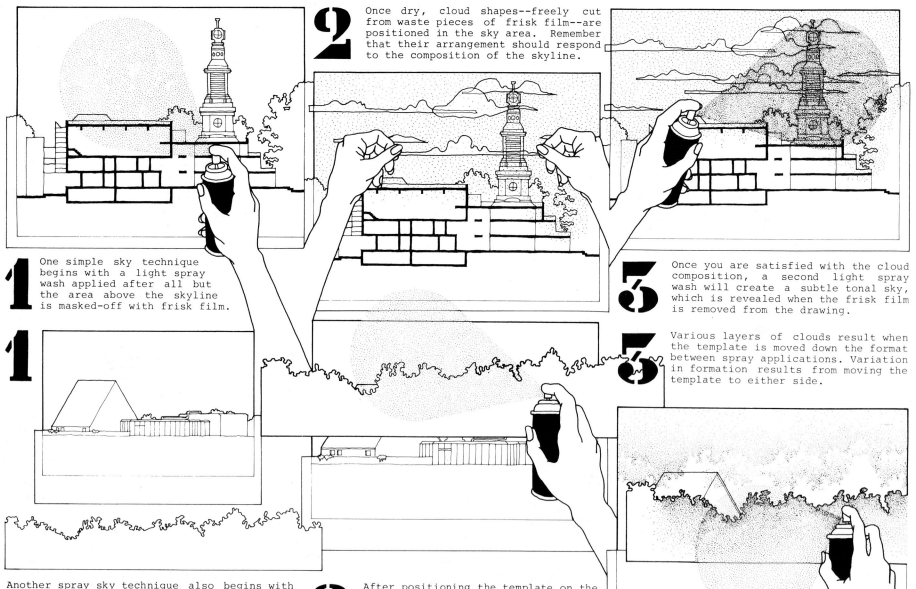

**2** Once dry, cloud shapes--freely cut from waste pieces of frisk film--are positioned in the sky area. Remember that their arrangement should respond to the composition of the skyline.

**1** One simple sky technique begins with a light spray wash applied after all but the area above the skyline is masked-off with frisk film.

**3** Once you are satisfied with the cloud composition, a second light spray wash will create a subtle tonal sky, which is revealed when the frisk film is removed from the drawing.

**3** Various layers of clouds result when the template is moved down the format between spray applications. Variation in formation results from moving the template to either side.

**1** Another spray sky technique also begins with all but the sky area masked with frisk film. This time a card template is cut or torn that, being wider than the drawing, offers a continuous cumulus cloud formation.

**2** After positioning the template on the exposed area of sky, apply a light wash, encouraging a more concentrated application along the undulating upper edge of the template.

# Graphite Dust Sky Technique

The medium for this sky technique is graphite dust collected from the bottom of a pointer. Graphite dust is useful for introducing atmospheric effects into elevations drawn in pencil or technical pen on tracing paper and opaque drawing boards. The graphite dust is worked in conjunction with a pliable kneaded "putty" eraser and a soft graphite pencil, such as a 6B. Graphite dust applicators include a pad of soft tissue paper, a cotton swab, and your forefinger.

Before application of the graphite dust, it is important to mask with frisk film the entire silhouette of the elevation skyline and, if required, around the upper and side borders. Then proceed to freely apply the graphite dust with the pad of tissue paper in response to a preplanned cloud composition. This technique is ideal for transparent drawings destined for diazo reproduction, which, to avoid a mess, can be worked on the reverse side of the drawing.

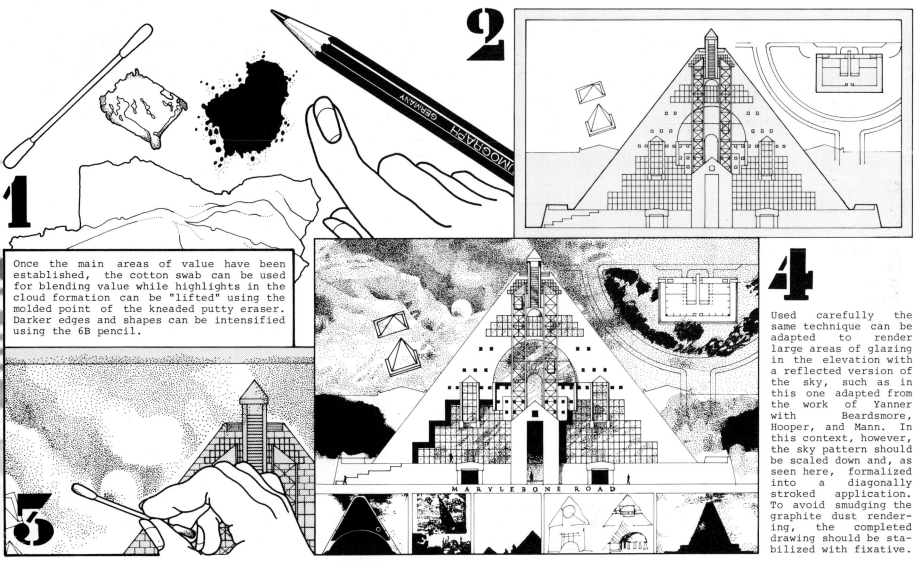

Once the main areas of value have been established, the cotton swab can be used for blending value while highlights in the cloud formation can be "lifted" using the molded point of the kneaded putty eraser. Darker edges and shapes can be intensified using the 6B pencil.

MARYLEBONE ROAD

Used carefully the same technique can be adapted to render large areas of glazing in the elevation with a reflected version of the sky, such as in this one adapted from the work of Yanner with Beardsmore, Hooper, and Mann. In this context, however, the sky pattern should be scaled down and, as seen here, formalized into a diagonally stroked application. To avoid smudging the graphite dust rendering, the completed drawing should be stabilized with fixative.

# Nighttime Skies

Designers will occasionally illustrate their perspectives, sections, and, particularly, elevations as an after-dark event. This is done either to demonstrate a nighttime activity or to explore and communicate the effects of electric lighting. Nighttime effects in such drawings can be achieved quickly by photographically reversing a black-on-white drawing. Alternatively, reversals can be achieved using a state-of-the-art photocopying machine. This conversion of regular ink on paper drawings into white-on-black images can bring some spectacular effects into night skies, such as searchlights, laser beams, and fireworks.

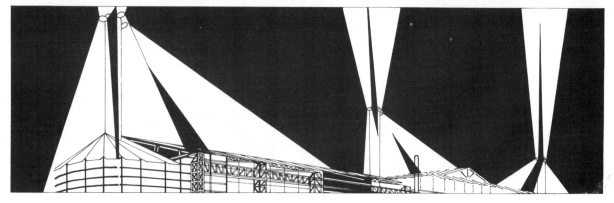

# Flying Entourage

Skies in elevations and perspectives can be given minor focal points by the insertion of various forms of aircraft. If not used to satisfy a whim of the designer, such aerial entourage can be incorporated as compositional devices to counterbalance large vertical skyline silhouettes, to draw attention to upper architectural features, or, especially in drawings with a strong horizontal emphasis, to make graphic connections between foreground and background events. Also, in simulating the pilot's point of view, the aerial perspective can employ flying objects, such as airplanes, to establish a sense of distance together with a reference point from which to view an architectural proposal. However, since such a decision places the flying object in the elevated foreground, drawings of aircraft should be kept simple, i.e., avoid any detail that might detract from the central architectural message.

The examples illustrated here begin with some fascinating flying objects seen over the Broadacre City Project designed by Frank Lloyd Wright in 1934 (above). Other more conventional craft include Norman Foster's helicopter (a), Robert MacDonald's RAF fighter planes (e), and Ron Herron's airship (g).

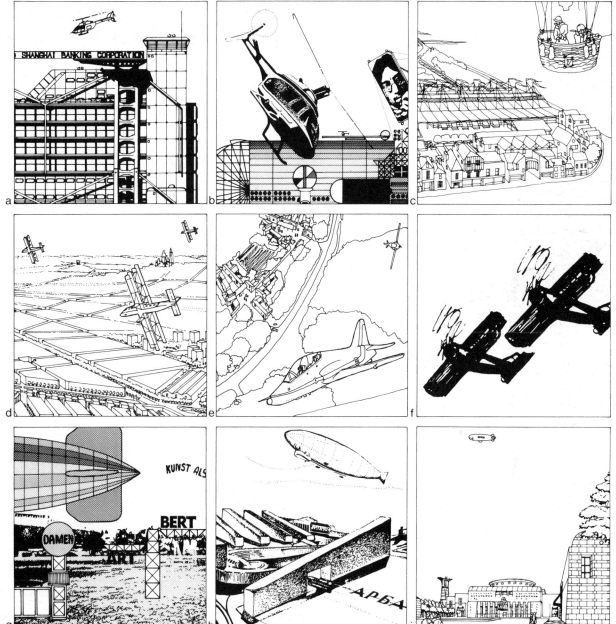

# Aerial Entourage

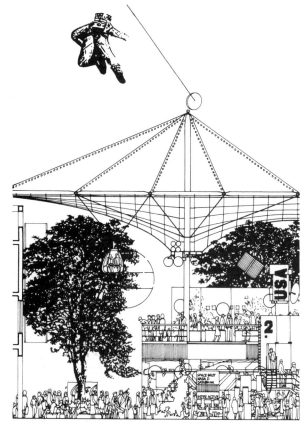

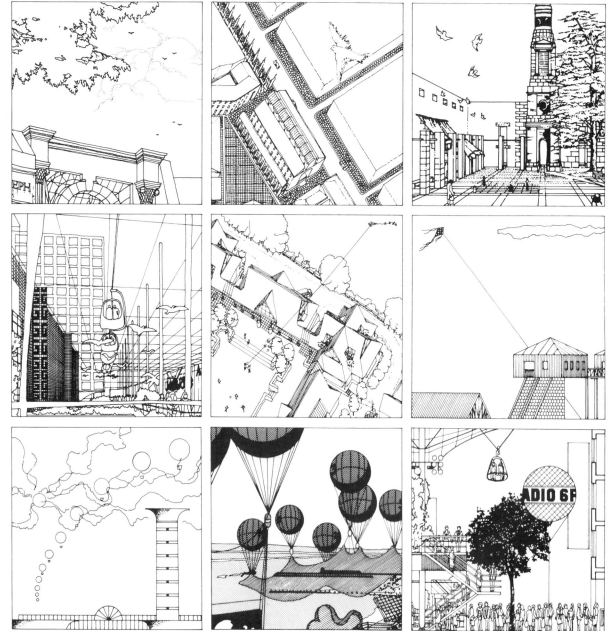

Other aerial entourage found in the skies of presentation drawings include hot-air balloons, kites, occasional flocks of birds, and, as we can see in the above section by Michael Hopkins, even free-fall parachutists! However, as we have already mentioned, indulgence in the detail of such entourage can be counterproductive when, especially in axonometrics, it might compromise the architectural content of the drawing. Otherwise, a survey of the minimal indication of aerial events in elevations and perspectives finds kites being flown to bring vertical or diagonal dimension to essentially horizontal facades and formations of birds and balloons being incorporated to counterpoint the incidence of strong vertical forms as well as to exploit a sense of depth, especially in the inherent flatness of elevations.

# Grounded Airplanes

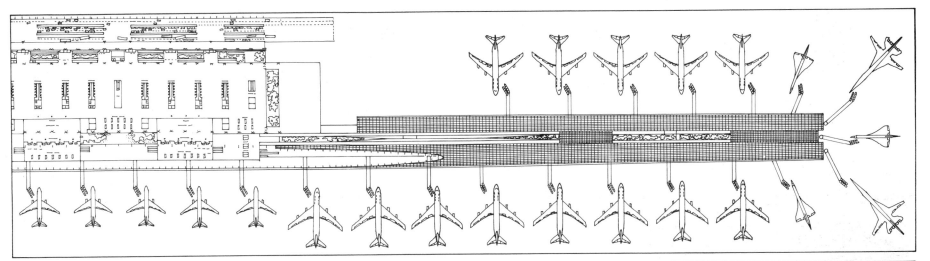

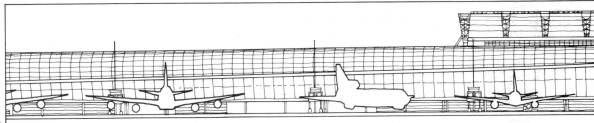

a

When grounded airplanes appear as repetitive
forms in large-scale plans, they are best
introduced in pressure transfer form. These
sheets offer several types of airplanes at
different scales, and their use is invaluable
for planning and testing runway, turning, and
docking allocation. In elevations, many
designers draw their own versions of airplanes against designs for terminal buildings. For instance, this elevation detail (a)
is taken--as is the plan (above)--from a
series of successful drawings entered for the
Kansai International Airport competition by
the office of Renzo Piano. In his elevation,
airplanes are simply outlined and drawn without an undercarriage to avoid overrestricting
the view through the building design. In complete contrast, the perspective drawing (b)
illustrates a more elaborate rendering of
foreground airplanes. Reminiscent of a prod-
uct designer's line and wash rendering technique, this drawing is taken from one by the
Scott Brownrigg & Turner practice of their
design for Southampton's Eastleigh Airport.

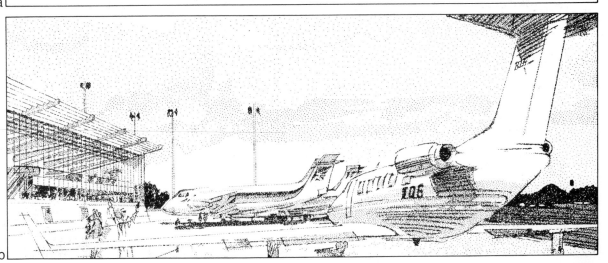

b

# Boats in Waterside Drawings

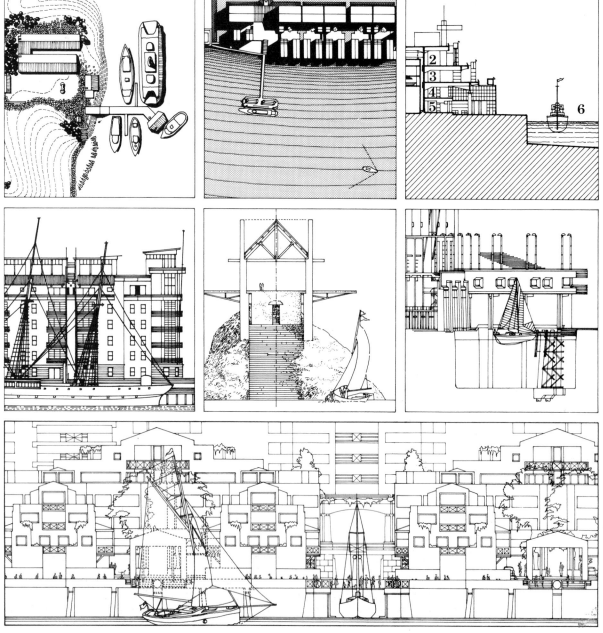

The opportunity to include boats in design proposals set in seaside, lakeside, riverside, and other water-related contexts should not be missed. Boats can bring to the design a sense of scale and romance, especially when they are moored alongside plans, elevations, and axonometrics, as well as occupy foreground or middle-distance vantage points from which to view perspectives. Being symmetrical, both plan and axonometric views rely on a center line around which the curve of boat forms are sensed--the axonometric view being constructed within a lightly ghosted crate.

# Boats in Waterside Drawings

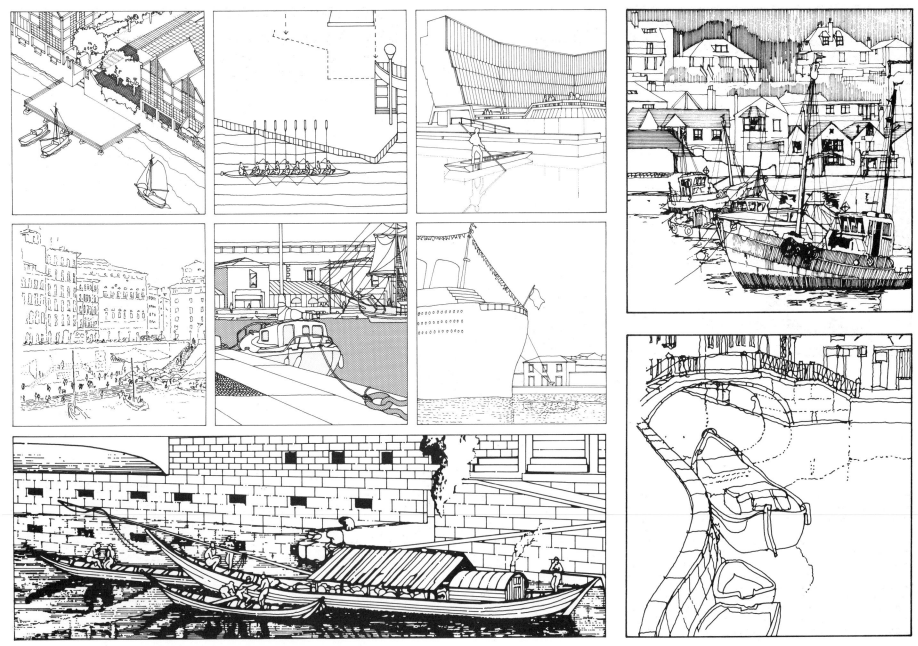

# Techniques for Water

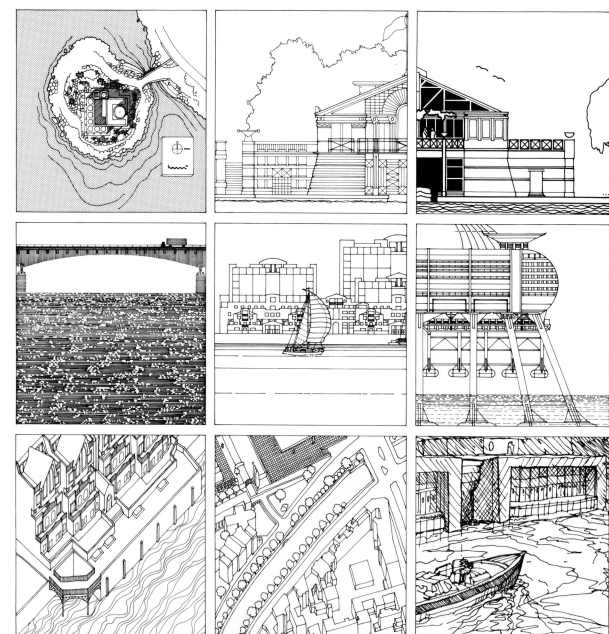

When not enlisted as a reflecting plane, the surface of water in most design drawings appears as a decorative stereotype. One common technique involves the familiar wavy line. Used either singly or in a series, it describes the horizontal profile of the water plane in sections or elevations, or hugs the banks and coastlines of small-scale landscape and site plans. Another technique uses a series of ruled and broken lines to simulate a rippled surface in strong sunlight. This is a very useful effect for creating sensations of depth in pseudo-perspectives--especially when, as shown, the lengths of line increase as they approach the viewer. A similar effect is also found in sections, but this time to describe a revealing slice through liquid mass for an underwater view.

# Reflections in Elevations and Axonometrics

Similarly, when plotting reflections in paraline drawings, the reflection is merely an inverted paraline projection of whatever is seen above the waterline. The extremities of the reflection, i.e., eaves or roofline, are found at the ends of wall projections that, once they have penetrated and taken account of the thickness of the horizontal plane remain at their same length.

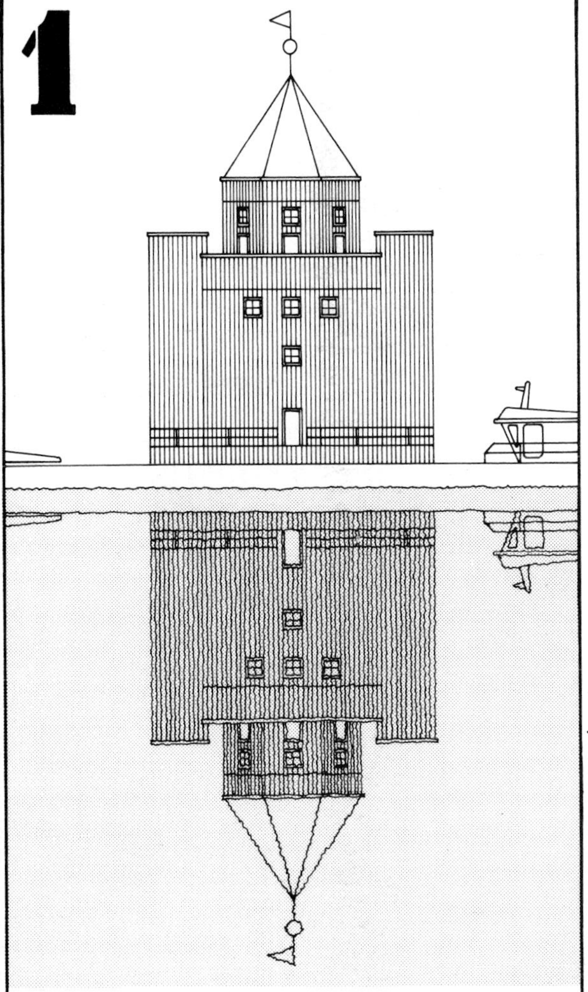

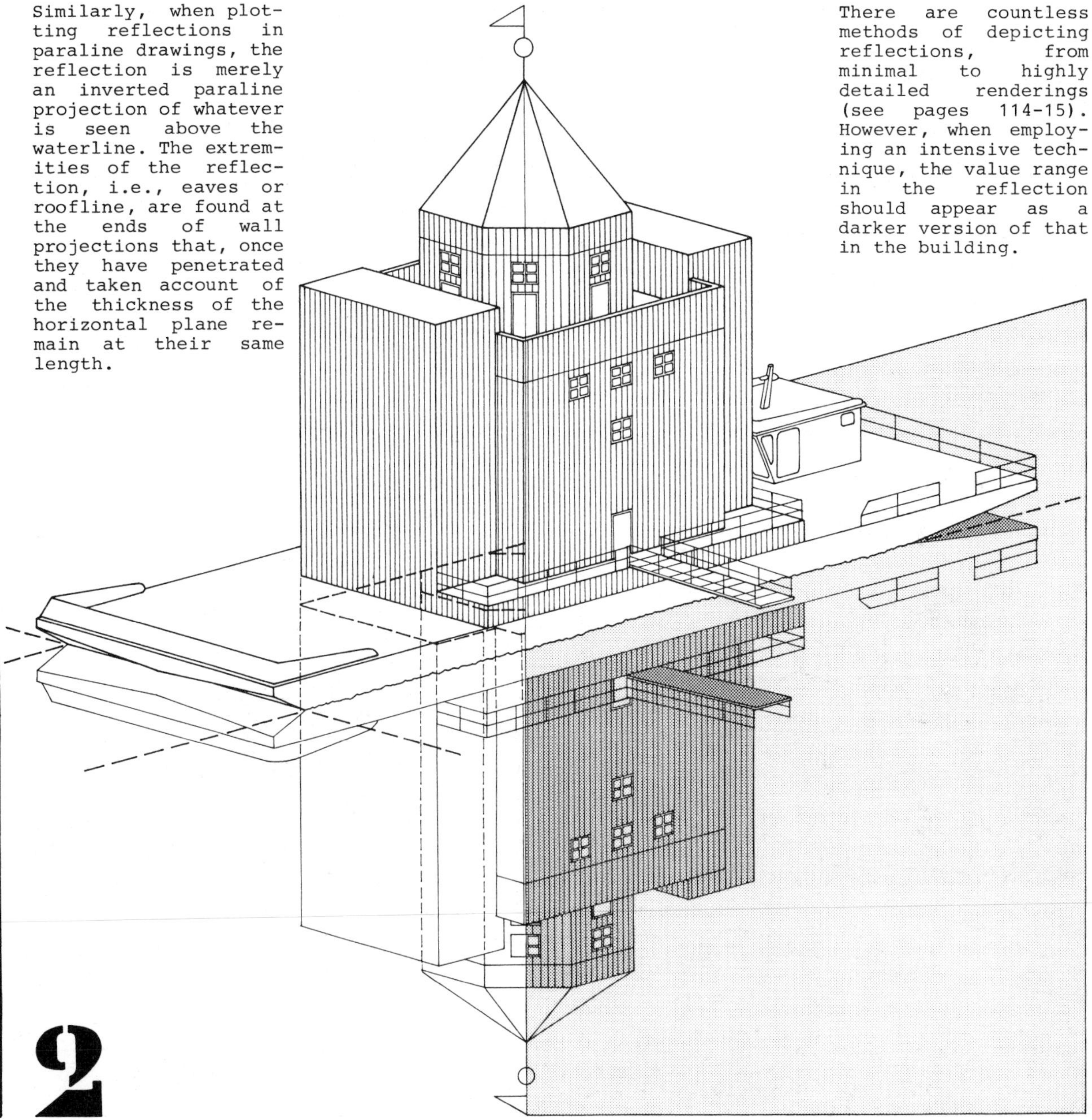

There are countless methods of depicting reflections, from minimal to highly detailed renderings (see pages 114-15). However, when employing an intensive technique, the value range in the reflection should appear as a darker version of that in the building.

Plotting reflections in elevations is quite simple. All that one has to remember is that, in representing the edge of the horizontal reflecting plane, the waterline is the key coordinate. Everything that appears above this line--including the thickness of the bank (the distance between the waterline and the ground line) --will appear in the same scale below as an inverted image.

**113**

# Techniques for Reflections in Water

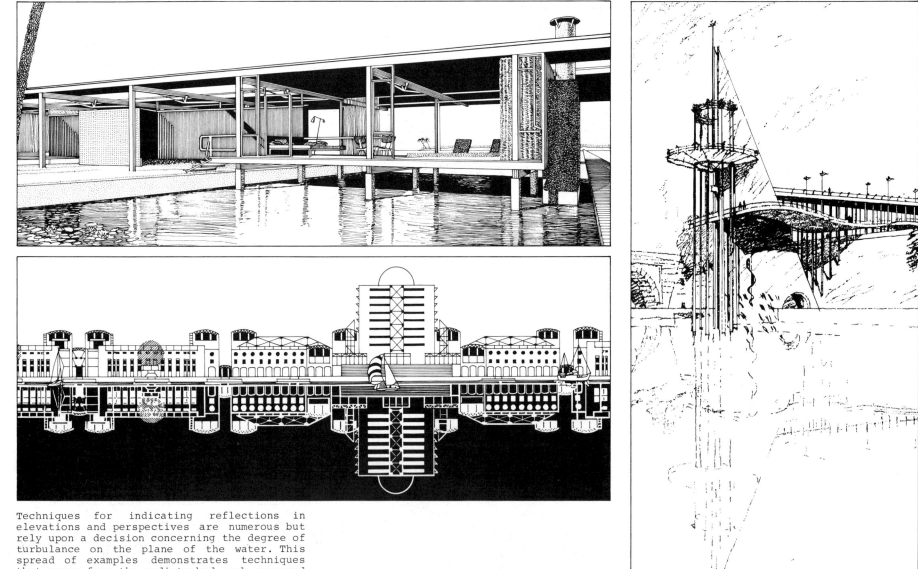

Techniques for indicating reflections in elevations and perspectives are numerous but rely upon a decision concerning the degree of turbulance on the plane of the water. This spread of examples demonstrates techniques that range from the undisturbed and reversed mirror reflection to those that simulate and suggest various degrees of chop. The techniques also reflect a variety of time spent in their execution--from minimal techniques to an intensive hatching.

**114**

# Techniques for Reflections in Water

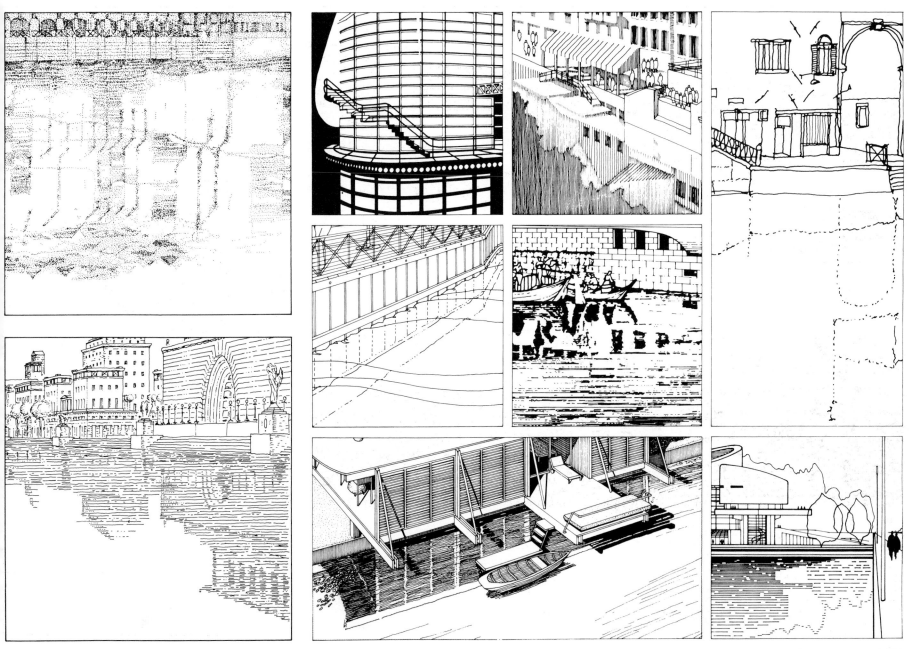

# Automobiles in Plans and Elevations

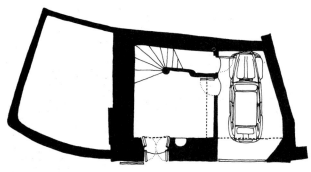

Just as with all types of orthographic entourage, the introduction of the automobile in plans acts as a check on the working function of large-scale plans. For instance, notice the conflict between the connecting door swing and the garaged car in the plan (above). Anomalies such as this are quickly highlighted when the designer deals directly with the way a space is to be used. In this case, a scaled pressure transfer graphic of an automobile has been inserted into a first-option ground-floor plan by Pancho Guedes.

The plan and elevational view of cars is comparatively easy to draw as they usually appear in such views exactly as they are often illustrated in manuals and ads. Down at the smaller scales of urban elevations and site sections, they can be quickly silhouetted in line or in solid black to bring a richness of texture as well as an indication of traffic movement. As they increase in scale, an outline profiling the body, doors, windshields, fenders, and wheels is usually sufficient to establish their presence without causing undue distraction. At the larger scales, automobile models become clearly identifiable, and a highly popular model that still appears, particularly in elevations, is the Volkswagen Beetle. This is possibly because the dynamic curve of its shape introduces a foil to the cubic profiles of building designs.

The incidence of automobiles and other vehicles in the space surrounding elevations and adjoining sections is quite common. Apart from adding contextual information, cars can signal the proximity of driveways, roads, and parking lots--usually unseen in these drawings--and convey something of their impact on the proposed architecture.

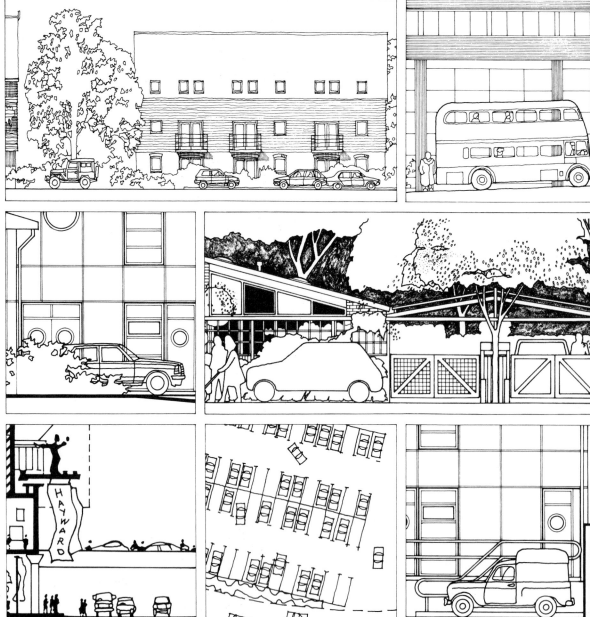

# Automobiles and Trucks in Axonometrics

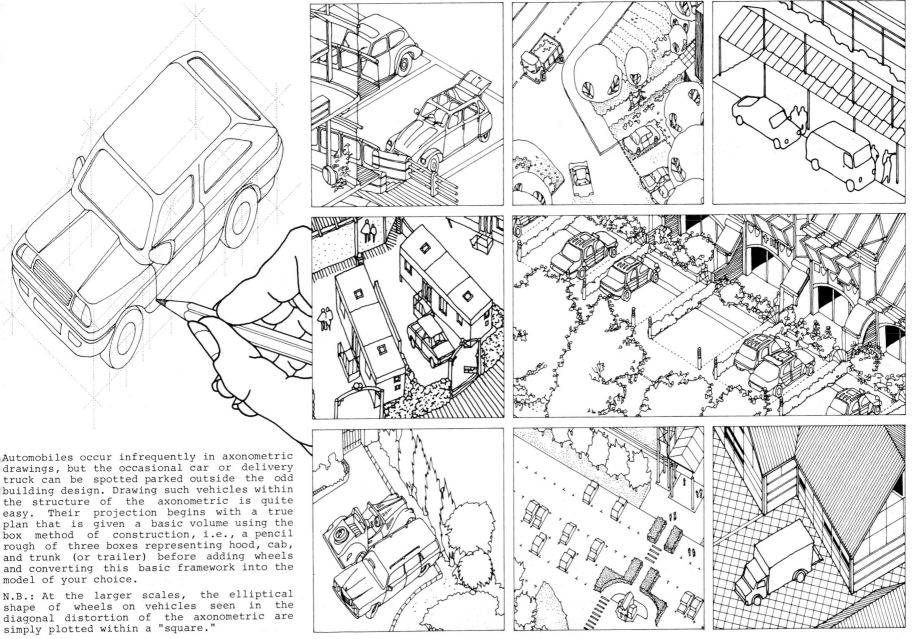

Automobiles occur infrequently in axonometric drawings, but the occasional car or delivery truck can be spotted parked outside the odd building design. Drawing such vehicles within the structure of the axonometric is quite easy. Their projection begins with a true plan that is given a basic volume using the box method of construction, i.e., a pencil rough of three boxes representing hood, cab, and trunk (or trailer) before adding wheels and converting this basic framework into the model of your choice.

N.B.: At the larger scales, the elliptical shape of wheels on vehicles seen in the diagonal distortion of the axonometric are simply plotted within a "square."

# Automobiles in Perspectives

As always, the best strategy is to keep the drawings of automobiles as simple as possible and avoid the obvious distraction of graphically "parking" a Ferrari in front of your building design. Instead, deploy transport as it would be seen in relation to your chosen view of the design and aim for accurate proportion of the more basic models. Also, render them minimally and in the spirit of the technique used elsewhere in the perspective. As stated previously, many designers will accomplish this by tracing the outlines or freehand drawing directly from appropriate views of automobiles found in illustrative material. An alternative for basic and characterless models is to use the "box" construction method mentioned on page 117 but harnessed to the vanishing point or points.

N.B.: Whether tracing automobiles from magazines or setting up their outlines from vanishing points, remember that the height of cars is lower than average eye level.

# Automobiles in Perspectives

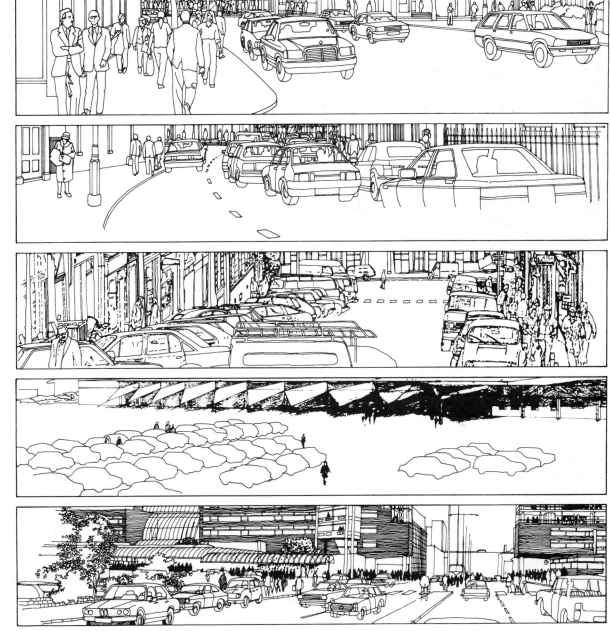

It is interesting to note that although both identifiable and characterless models of drawn automobiles occur in design drawings, those found in our survey of presentation perspectives tended to be of the former type. There are two basic techniques used when representing recognizable cars. The first illustrates the car in an outline that generalizes the main components of the body with, especially in those that approach the foreground, a line to profile the driver. The other technique simplifies the automobile with a line that silhouettes the outer shape --a method employed when the architectural message needs to be dominant. This particular technique is ideal for showing the impact of parking lot layouts in use. Common to all these drawings is the use of both automobiles and pedestrians--a combination that helps to retain a check on the scale of the vehicles and their relationship with the space they occupy.

# Entourage in Action

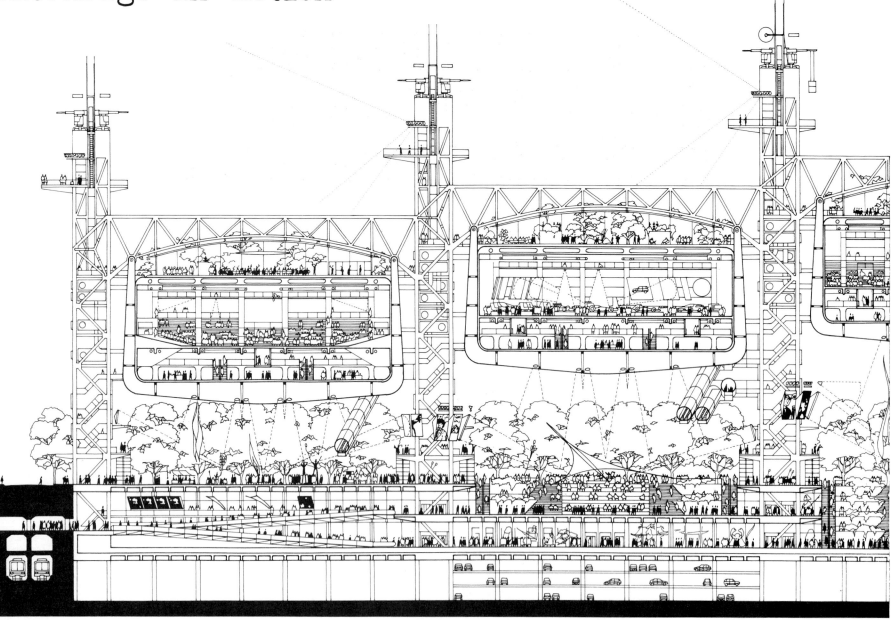

This visually stunning and highly animated section--produced as part of an entry for the Tokyo Forum competition by Richard Rogers & Partners--takes full advantage of the vast majority of entourage elements covered in this book.  In so doing, this skillfully drafted design drawing becomes rich in information; it allows the building to come alive and to be viewed as a working mechanism.

# 6 LETTERING, LABELING, AND LAYOUT

# An Introduction to Lettering

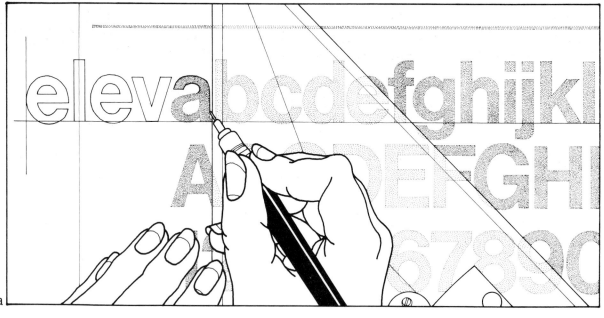

a

b

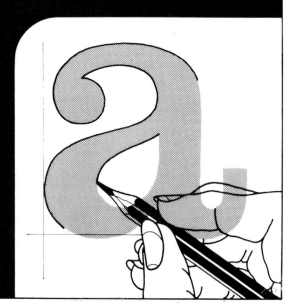

c

Traditionally taught mainly through the construction principles of roman letterforms, the teaching of lettering has long since vanished from courses in environmental design. Meanwhile, many designers in a hurry settle for a rather comic, freehand version of block lettering--a lettering style peculiar to architectural and urban design drawings (above). However, rather than inventing a debased form of lettering, it is better to base freehand letterforms on the integrity of a recognized source. A good and economical way of doing this is to photocopy a range of alphabets from sheets or catalogues of dry-transfer lettering. These can then be enlarged or reduced on a photocopier before being used as tracing guides for lettering titles in drawings on transparent materials (a). Alternatively, when working on opaque materials, letterforms can be trace-transferred using carbon paper or by rubbing soft-grade graphite over each required character (b). Larger letterforms can be projected into position for tracing using an episcope (c).

**122**

An Introduction to Lettering

**Plan Elevation Section 1:20**

**Perspective Axonometric 1:5**

Plan Elevation Section 1:200

Perspective Axonometric 1:5

PLAN ELEVATION SECTION 1:200

PERSPECTIVE AXONOMETRIC 1:5

**PLAN ELEVATION SECTION 1:200**

**PERSPECTIVE AXONOMETRIC 1:5**

**PLAN ELEVATION SECTION 1:20**

**PERSPECTIVE AXONOMETRIC 1:5**

When selecting lettering, excessively modish styles should be avoided. Instead, choose typefaces that will communicate clearly without imposing their own design or style statements. Popular and "timeless" examples include Helvetica Medium, Microgramma Medium Extended, Roman, Clarendon, and the box stencil letterforms popularized by Eileen Gray and her mentor, Le Corbusier.

# Lettering in Design Drawings

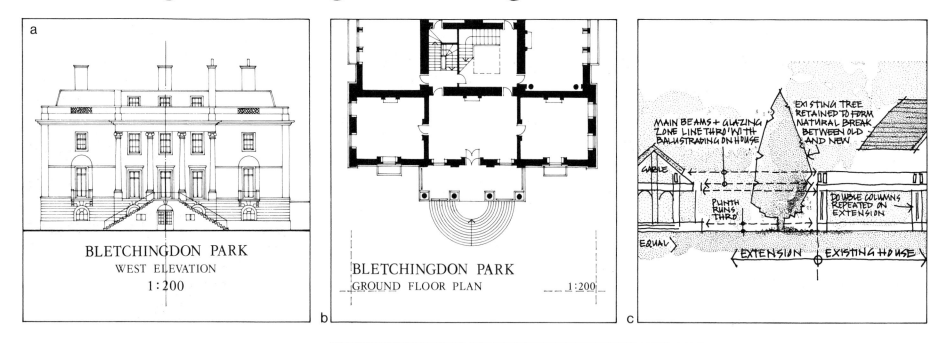

a

BLETCHINGDON PARK
WEST ELEVATION
1:200

b

BLETCHINGDON PARK
GROUND FLOOR PLAN                    1:200

c

MAIN BEAMS + GLAZING
ZONE LINE THRO' WITH
BALUSTRADING ON HOUSE

EXISTING TREE
RETAINED TO FORM
NATURAL BREAK
BETWEEN OLD
AND NEW

GABLE

PLINTH
RUNS
THRO'

DOUBLE COLUMNS
REPEATED ON
EXTENSION

EQUAL

EXTENSION        EXISTING HOUSE

When approached as a design component,
lettering can perform several functions in an
architectural drawing. For example, titles
can act as visual "plinths" (a) or as
restraining "frames" (b) within the composition of a layout, or they may be used as a
transitional element between other graphic
elements (c). Lettering should also find its
own scale in a presentation without appearing
either too mean or assuming an oversized
proportion that might distract attention from
the attendant drawing (d). One way to select
size is simply to see how a particular face
looks when viewed from the predicted distance
that the drawing will be viewed from.

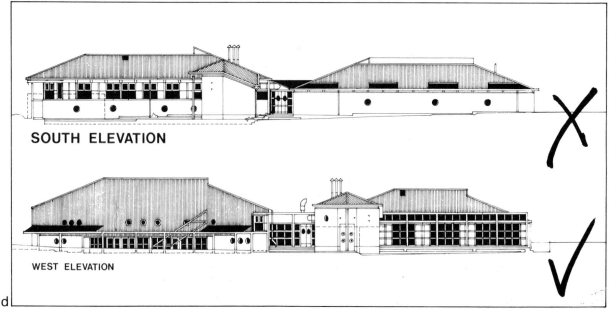

**SOUTH ELEVATION**

**WEST ELEVATION**

d

# Lettering in Design Drawings

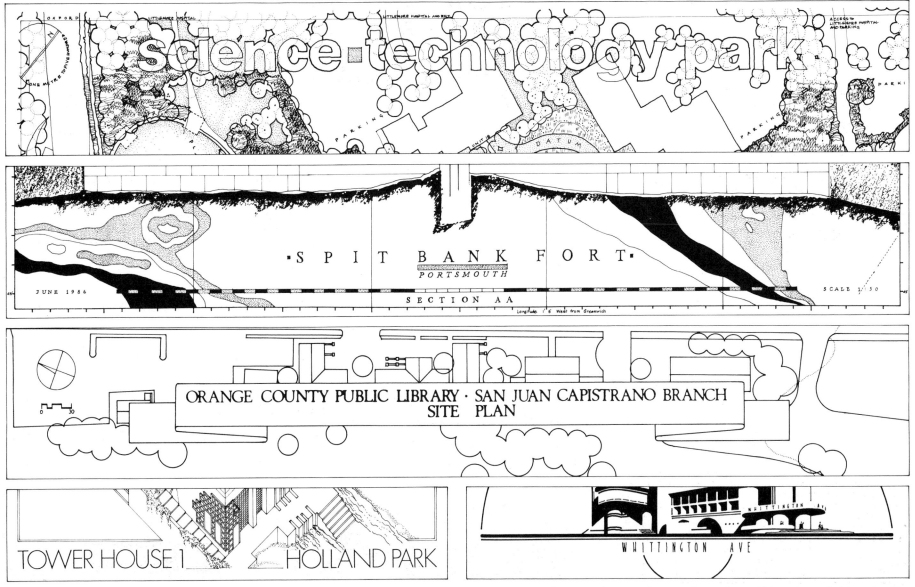

Here, we illustrate a selection of titles culled from a range of design drawings. Each title block appears to have been chosen with care and has been incorporated into its respective layout as a design element. For example, all are based on or are variations of classic typefaces. Also, each occupies a planned position in relation to the referent drawing without distracting from its size or technique. Indeed, in the first example the main title attempts an integration with the drawing itself.

# Annotating Design Drawings

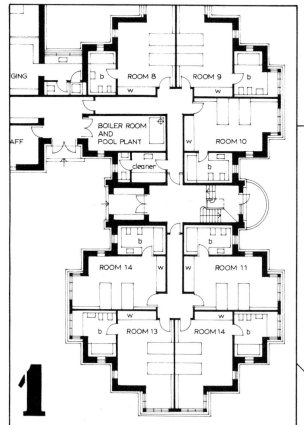

A good use of lettering will not only give information but will improve the overall presentation as well. At the smaller scales of lettering, many architects will develop a personal style of hand lettering that exists simply as a refined version of a handwriting style. For the best results, beginners should construct lettering between two horizontal guidelines, or, when using transparent materials, employ a graphed underlay.

A GOOD USE OF LETTERING WILL NOT ONLY GIVE INFORMATION BUT WILL IMPROVE THE OVERALL PRESENTATION AS WELL. AT THE SMALLER SCALES OF LETTERING, MANY ARCHITECTS WILL DEVELOP A PERSONAL STYLE OF HAND LETTERING THAT EXISTS SIMPLY AS A REFINED VERSION OF A HANDWRITING STYLE. FOR THE BEST RESULTS, BEGINNERS SHOULD CONSTRUCT LETTERING BETWEEN TWO HORIZONTAL GUIDELINES, ...

**1**

Many architectural drawings will require that lettering be organized both inside and around the area occupied by the graphic. In such drawings main titles should read in conjunction with the whole sheet while subtitles and labels should be legible without interfering with the drawing itself. When required, the labeling of various rooms or zones within, say, a plan or a section should be inserted to appear as an integrated part of the space they annotate. For instance, the size of this lettering should not be overbearing, and, whether the room shape is regular or irregular, should be positioned at its visual center of gravity or be located in a position that is consistent throughout the drawing.

...OR, WHEN USING TRANSPARENT MATERIALS, EMPLOY A GRAPHED UNDERLAY.

**2**

Straight strokes made with Ching's technical pen leave characteristic blobs at the beginning and ending of strokes. To maintain this handmade look, stroke terminals were left more irregular and natural. A careful balance was established between the uniformity of strokes and letterspacing, and the lively irregularity of shapes and alignments.

The design process included many iterations, modifications, and adjustments. Siegel and the Adobe type design staff carefully studied output from laser printers and digital typesetters at numerous point sizes to evaluate lettershape, design, and spacing.

To add to the usefulness of this package, a slightly inclined oblique font is included. The design is a slanted version of the roman font. Tekton Oblique can be an ideal complement to Tekton Regular, or it can be dynamic and attractive when used alone. A large number of kerning pairs is provided so that the typeface can more closely approximate the look of Ching's hand-lettering.

The utilitarian simplicity of the Tekton typeface lends itself to computer-aided design, engineering drawing, and architectural applications. Its informal character makes it useful for correspondence, proposals, and invitations. In the hands of the creative and skillful designer, Tekton font software has unlimited potential.

A familiar style of hand lettering is that developed by the architect and writer Frank Ching. After being used successfully throughout his books, Ching's particular clarity of style has been elevated to recognition as a standard typeface. This results from its adoption in the Adobe Systems range of computer font software as "tekton" for application to engineering and architectural drawings. However, a study of Ching's distinctive letter formation and spacing functions as an excellent model for those who seek perfection.

# Annotating Design Drawings

An efficient method of annotating complex design drawings produced at the smaller scales is to stack written information into blocks to either side or above the drawing. Used in this way, columns of lettering function both as blocks of information and as basic design elements--individual labels being keyed into their graphic counterparts with thin lines to avoid confusion. An alternative method is the annotation of drawings using numerals. Each number located on the drawing refers the viewer to a legend that, within the overall layout, is clearly located in relation to its parent image (see page 129).

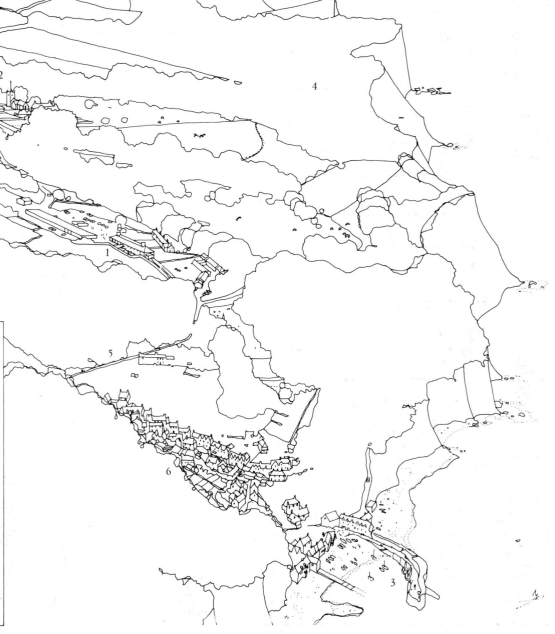

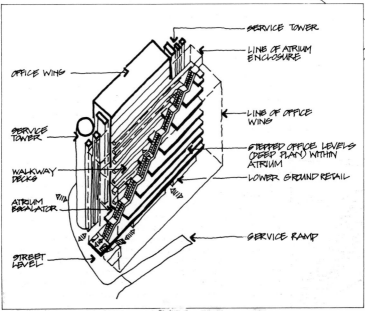

# Graphic Continuity

The relationship between the style of a design proposal and the character of lettering is another important consideration. For instance, being viewed as timeless in appearance, typefaces, such as Roman and Helvetica Medium, become universally used in design drawings and, indeed, in the built environment. When branching out into other characters--and when graphic consistency is your goal--care should be taken to marry the style of lettering with the style of the design. For example, see if you agree with each of the letterfaces below in relation to their meaning.

**Classical**

GOTHIC

**Baroque**

EDWARDIAN

*Art Nouveau*

**ART DECO**

International

**Helvetica** Medium

**Clarendon** Medium

Optima

**Futura** Bold

*Avant Garde Gothic* X-Light

Univers 53

**Futura** Black

The stylistic relationship between lettering and northpoint in plans is an issue raised by Professor Sarah Recken of Washington University. She proposes that, since well-designed alphabets are hallmarked by a recognizable consistency of form, boldness, and style, the selected letterform for headings and titling, etc., should dictate the design of the arrow. She illustrates this quest for graphic consistency in the examples shown here.

# The Legend

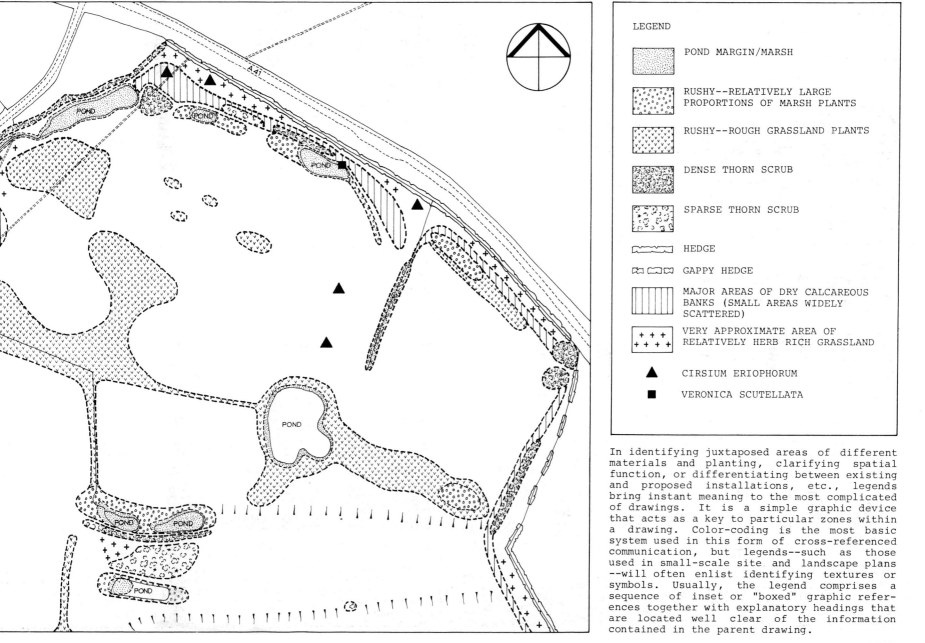

LEGEND

POND MARGIN/MARSH

RUSHY--RELATIVELY LARGE PROPORTIONS OF MARSH PLANTS

RUSHY--ROUGH GRASSLAND PLANTS

DENSE THORN SCRUB

SPARSE THORN SCRUB

HEDGE

GAPPY HEDGE

MAJOR AREAS OF DRY CALCAREOUS BANKS (SMALL AREAS WIDELY SCATTERED)

VERY APPROXIMATE AREA OF RELATIVELY HERB RICH GRASSLAND

▲ CIRSIUM ERIOPHORUM

■ VERONICA SCUTELLATA

In identifying juxtaposed areas of different materials and planting, clarifying spatial function, or differentiating between existing and proposed installations, etc., legends bring instant meaning to the most complicated of drawings. It is a simple graphic device that acts as a key to particular zones within a drawing. Color-coding is the most basic system used in this form of cross-referenced communication, but legends--such as those used in small-scale site and landscape plans --will often enlist identifying textures or symbols. Usually, the legend comprises a sequence of inset or "boxed" graphic references together with explanatory headings that are located well clear of the information contained in the parent drawing.

# Signage in Buildings

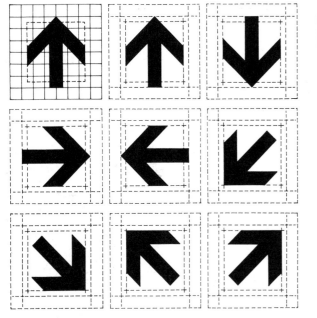

Signage appears in all kinds of public build-ings--from shopping malls, offices, airports, parking lots, to sports facilities and tem-porary events, such as World's Fairs and the Olympic Games. Graphic systems for public spaces have been the subject of numerous international attempts to establish standards for a set of symbols that might best orien-tate pedestrians and passengers. In 1981, the American Institute of Graphic Arts prepared a total system of orientation symbols based on a study of earlier and existing systems for the U.S. Department of Transportation. Here are some of their symbols beginning with a directional arrow (above) designed to complement the style and proportions of their recommended signs.

# Signage in Buildings

When included in design drawings, communication systems involving lettering, signs, and symbols are either an afterthought or merely trivialized. This is because, like landscape and interior design, the architect sometimes regards graphic design as a specialism outside his or her domain and, consequently, avoids these issues in the design process. Therefore, the drawings shown here are rarities in that they attempt to depict the impact of directional and commercial signage on the proposed design of public space.

When including informational graphics in design drawings, the key is to avoid both a confusion of information and a sterility of image. For example, directional signage should be designed to register simply and clearly. Rather than mixing insignificant with essential messages, it should reserve the use of symbols for the most important information. Other examples of signage in buildings occur on pages 51 and 63.

# Lettering on Buildings

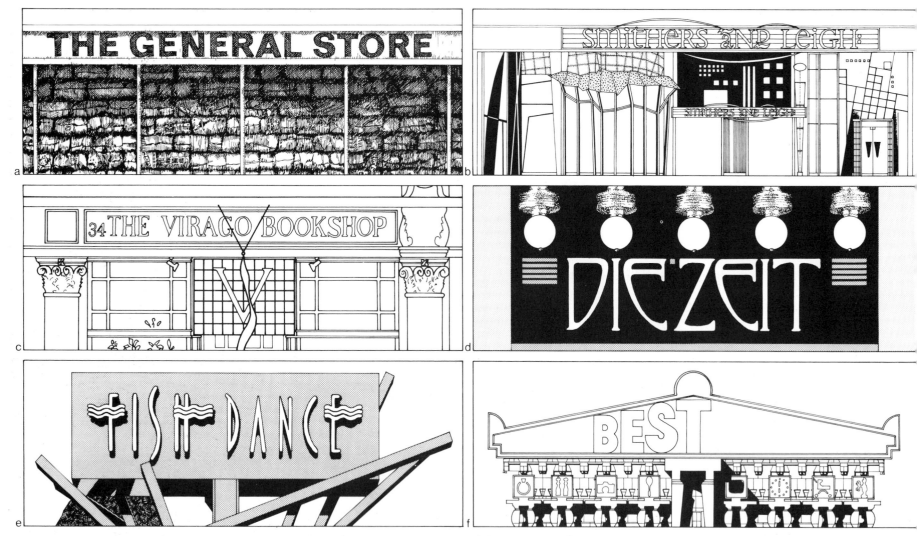

Although the experience of lettering on buildings is an everyday aspect of our perception of the built environment, it is curious that it is generally ignored in the design process--its occasional appearance apparently resulting as an afterthought. Therefore, it is worth digressing momentarily to examine the potential of lettering in this context. As a design element, lettering can, by itself, provide the double function of form and symbol. For instance, the selection of letter form in an elevation by the Site design group says "The General Store," but its style symbolizes simplicity and timelessness

(a). Conversely, the symbolism behind the Crighton design group's intentionally discordant mixture of upper- and lowercase roman letter forms set against a cacophony of facade elements becomes more relevant when we realize that this is their design proposal for the entrance to a music store (b). The selection, sizing, and positioning of lettering for buildings is an important aspect of architectural design. Each of these examples represent faces--either found or custom designed--that fulfill the dual roles of form and symbol on the facades of commercial buildings.

# Lettering on Buildings

There are several examples of building designs in which letter forms play a key architectural role. Such an example is the penthouse-level addition--together with a skyline sign--proposed by Terry Farrell for London's Savoy Hotel (b). In his proposal, the choice of letterform echoes the period of the existing building as well as reflects the decorative elements in the fenestration, such as the repetition of the "V" and the "Y." Another example of large-scale lettering, this time by Robert Venturi, is the roman letterform for the Seattle Art Museum, which becomes integrated with the vertical rhythms of the main facade of his proposed design for that building (a). Here, each letter plays its part as an element in an overall pattern of facade events that, rather than appear as an afterthought, is totally integrated into the elevation. Finally, to complete our mini-excursion into architectural lettering, we should consider letterforms as the generator of architectural form. For instance, in this detail taken from a drawing by Peter Cook and Christine Hawley, the three letters of the German DOM lock company physically form the main elevation and the roof profile that determines the overall form of the structure (c).

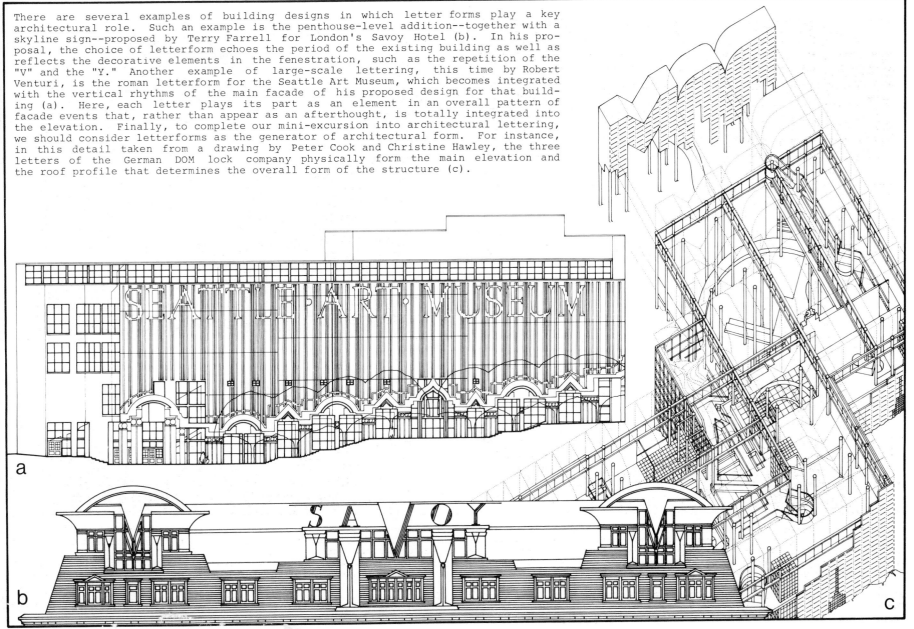

# An Introduction to Layout

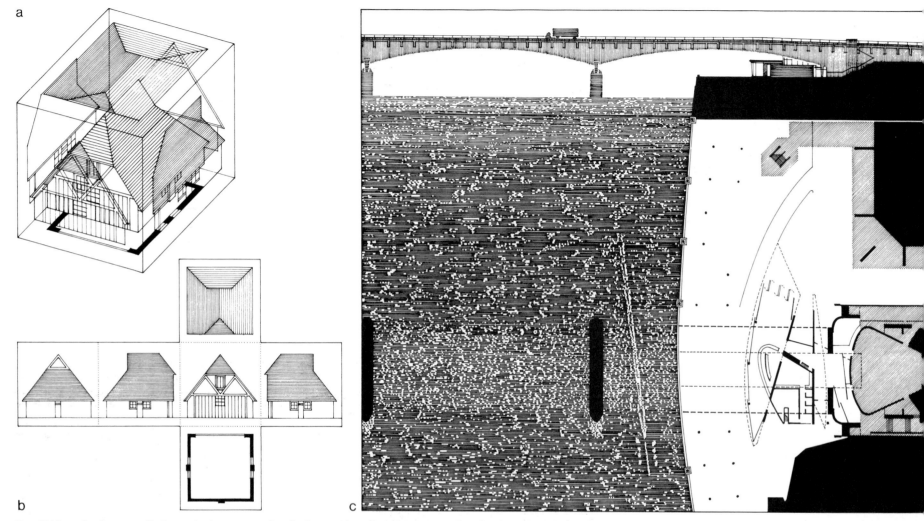

a

b

c

Traditional forms of layout have evolved from the development of first angle projection. This convention sees an architectural design as visualized within a "glass box," with the significant faces of the conceptual form as projected onto the inside of the glass in "first angle projection," or the outside of the glass in "third angle projection" (a). When conceptually opened flat, the layout, depending on the convention used, places the plan either above or below its elevations. The resulting arrangement of scaled and dimensionally related orthographic views combine to provide a coordinated picture of all the information required to comprehend and mentally reconstruct the appearance of the form in question (b). However, many designers will devise their own layouts and even tailor a different layout for each individual project. In contrast to traditional layout, the influence of the restricted entry format of international design competitions and their widespread publication has caused designers to experiment with variations on traditional layout. As a result of the designer's need to catch the judges' eye in preliminary rounds of selection, more dynamic and adventurous forms of layout have evolved. These are characterized by variation in the scale of orthographics and the squeezing together, overlapping, and layering of graphic information within the format. Such layouts are carefully planned and are reminiscent of how an artist might plan an abstract composition (c).

# An Introduction to Layout

a

b

c

LAND WARFARE HALL · IMPERIAL WAR MUSEUM · DUXFORD

1 50 SECTION ALONG CENTRAL SPINE

PERSPECTIVE

Rather than be left to chance, presentation layouts should be preplanned as a total composition. This organizational approach necessitates the gathering together of all the graphic components required to clearly communicate the design in question. Layout development can employ a series of trial-and-error thumbnail sketches that, worked against the framework of a background grid, aim to orchestrate each graphic component into an overall composition (a). However, depending on the complexity of the design and its selected scale, or range of scales, an early decision needs to be made regarding the use of sheets in the overall format. For example, will the layout comprise a series of individually composed and self-contained sheets that, when displayed as a set, are intended to be viewed separately and sequentially (b)? Or will the layout be devised as an independent composition that occupies an overall format provided by several sheets (c)? This basic decision returns us to the spirit of the design idea and the roles of the different drawing types enlisted within the design sequence (see page 136).

see page 136

# Key Drawings in Layout Design

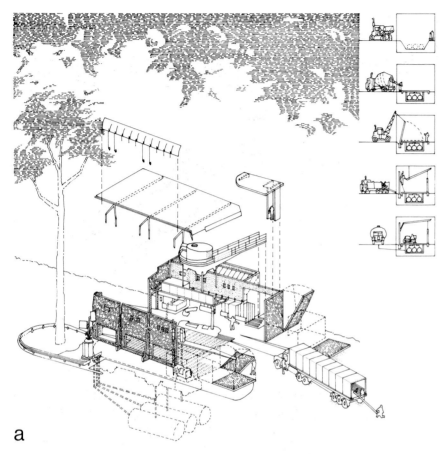

a

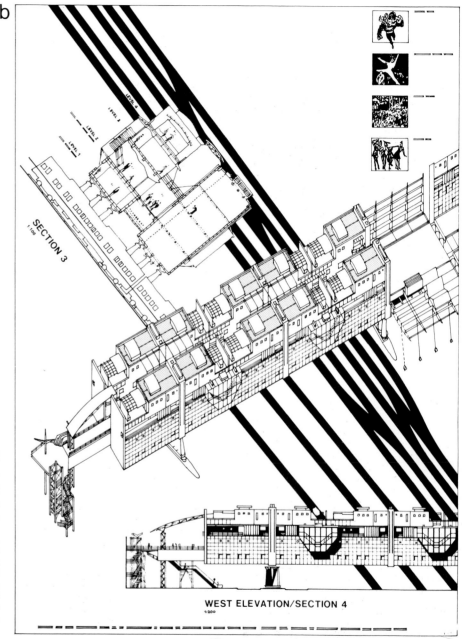

Each layout is adapted to the uniqueness of each design project and is generated by the range of drawing types needed to adequately describe its complexity. Also, within a layout design, certain types of drawing may be modified in order to fulfill specific communication roles (see pages 138-39). However, the emergence of the key drawing as the central communication vehicle in the presentation usually involves the recycling of a graphic type that has already proven its worth in summarizing the concept earlier in the design sequence. Indeed, the extensively published key drawings of many well-known buildings are more widely known than their physical counterparts--one key drawing often capturing the essence of an architectural intent and, through media exposure, becoming a mental icon "visited" and "revisited" in the mind's eye (a). Having been identified as the best graphic model to describe the design, this drawing type can be employed on a large scale and function as the referential centerpiece of a layout against which smaller scale and subordinated information can be arranged (b).

# Key Drawings in Layout Design

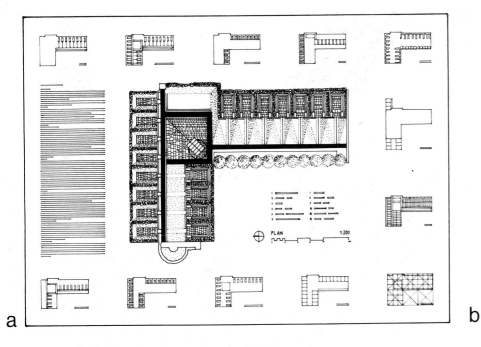

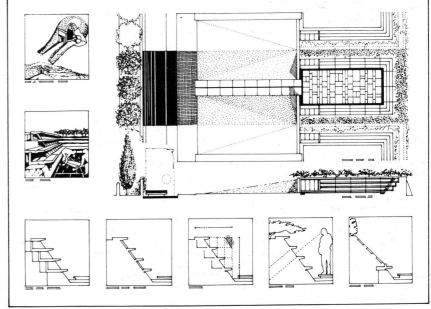

These three sheet layouts by John Pardey and Ronald Yee, two consistently successful competition entrants, represent the joint premier prize-winning entry for a competition to design a cemetery. They demonstrate the impact of a clear, consistent, and visually accessible design statement arranged around a simple grid layout. Each sheet fronts with its own key drawing as centerpiece, and each is framed in different ways by supplementary and smaller scaled information. For instance, including its floorscape and planting, the plan is surrounded on three sides with a "frame" of diagrammatic plans that communicate analytically the potential of the design (a). Notice that in this layout the "frame" is completed by a block of text outlining the objectives of the design scheme. Notice also that the legend, northpoint, and graphic scale are composed into another block positioned so as to complete the inner "invisible" rectangle formed by the central plan. Meanwhile, in the next sheet, the isometric centerpiece is braced at the top by a series of selected perspective drawings that takes us on a tour of the proposed space (b). Finally, the third sheet presents an amplified detail of the masterplan, together with its attendant longitudinal section (c). Again, this graphic combination is "framed," this time on two sides, with, first, a design precedent, followed by a sequence of diagrammatic sections conveying various options for details.

# Progressive Assembly Graphic as Key Drawing

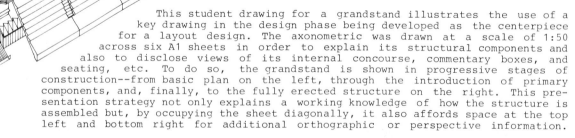

This student drawing for a grandstand illustrates the use of a key drawing in the design phase being developed as the centerpiece for a layout design. The axonometric was drawn at a scale of 1:50 across six A1 sheets in order to explain its structural components and also to disclose views of its internal concourse, commentary boxes, and seating, etc. To do so, the grandstand is shown in progressive stages of construction--from basic plan on the left, through the introduction of primary components, and, finally, to the fully erected structure on the right. This presentation strategy not only explains a working knowledge of how the structure is assembled but, by occupying the sheet diagonally, it also affords space at the top left and bottom right for additional orthographic or perspective information.

# Exploded Graphic as Key Drawing

This drawing of a student design for the conversion of a nineteenth-century brick and masonry pergola into a restaurant is another example of the axonometric functioning as the centerpiece of a layout. In proving itself in the design process, this drawing explodes its roofdeck and suspended ceiling to disclose the dining area, lobby, and bar. In its presented form the axonometric fills two A1 sheets and is framed horizontally above and below with a string of small boxed images that explain site location, modifications to existing elevation, and details of furniture, lighting, and fittings, etc.

# Layout as Storyboard

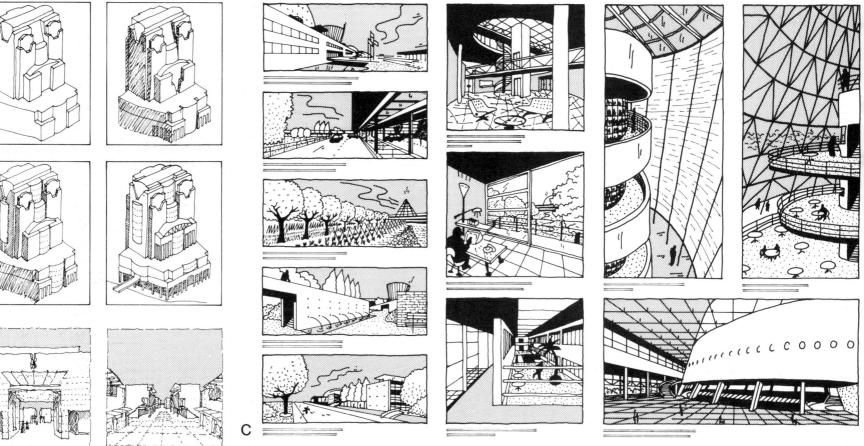

a

Entrance from piazza through colonnaded four and five storey commercial block.

The internal court is landscaped or open for parking with loggias occasionally offering shelter. Pavilions mark a gateway beyond.

BLOCK B
SEQUENCE THROUGH BLOCKS

Four storey pavilions offer a smaller scale to the opposing commercial blocks. They contain smaller artisan workshops and look out towards the quay.

The quayside is inhabited by cafés and other social activities. Glimpses of public buildings and loggias add to the illusion of activity.

b

c

A good way of approaching layout design is from the standpoint of storytelling. In other words, the layout is designed to reflect a predetermined storyline that communicates the design concept in a logical disclosure of information. This approach can adopt one of two basic narratives. On the one hand, the layout could simply tell the story of the design proposal. On the other hand, a more persuasive strategy "narrates" the entire design route from conception to final design. In a condensed form, the latter is common in competition layouts that, by their very nature, are viewed away from the presence of their designers and can, for example, include design precedents --that is, the influential sources of inspiration, design details, and perspective sequences, etc. This kind of strategy generally utilizes serial images, or comic-strip boxes of information, that, in layout terms, can double-function to frame a key drawing (see page 137) or exist in their own right. For instance, the series of frames on the left are taken from various layouts, each storyboarding a different aspect of their designs (a, b). Meanwhile, the block of perspectives on the right perform a valuable function at the climax of a layout. They are taken from the award-winning work of Dutch designers W. J. Neutelings and F. R. Roodbeen, who produced them as part of their submission for the new European Patent Office design competition. In taking the viewer on a visual "tour" around exterior, interior, and courtyard spaces, these serial drawings animate their design proposal in an exciting and persuasive fashion (c).

# Layout as Storyboard

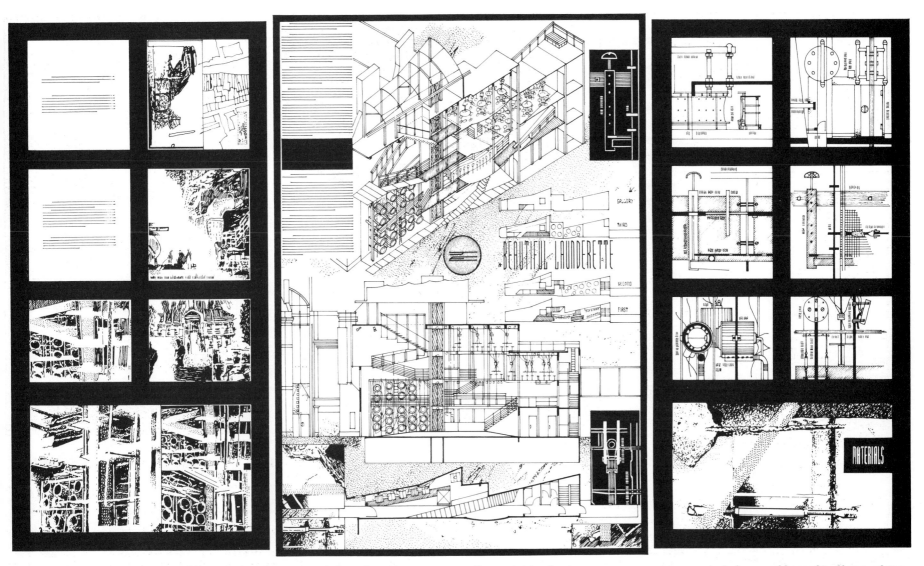

This student interior design project for a new launderette uses a group of three associated picture panels, i.e., a triptych format, to "storyboard" a short history of the design sequence. The left-hand panel introduces sources that influenced the scheme (sets from the movies Bladerunner and Metropolis) together with photographs of the working model from which the interior was initially developed. The central panel carries a prominant section--which featured strongly in the graphic design sequence--accompanied by small-scale floor plans, shopfront elevation, and street elevation--to communicate its context. To complete the three-part story of the layout, the third panel comprises white-on-black working drawings of critical details above a color photocopy (in the original) of a montage of actual materials intended for use in the launderette interior.

# "Stageset" Layouts

The fashion for assembling orthographics and perspectives into composite layouts that form their own space has evolved directly from the format restrictions imposed by international competitions. Both of these schemes illustrate how the graphic components of an architectural idea can be organized almost theatrically into a space created by the drawing types themselves. The layout on the left is the work of French architect Henri Ciriani. The perspective of the facade functions as the key drawing; its immediate foreground being used as a link through to the axonometric view at the bottom and also as a background for two additional, overlapping perspectives. A similar "stageset" layering of information is found in the more formal layout on the right by Rob Krier with Francy Valentiny and Hubert Ackmann. Here, an elevation backdrops a key perspective above a part-plan part-elevation while the site plan lies "hidden" in the landscape. Traditionalists might find such layouts contrived and confusing, but there is no doubt that such presentations are becoming more widespread among those who seek prizes and publication.

**142**

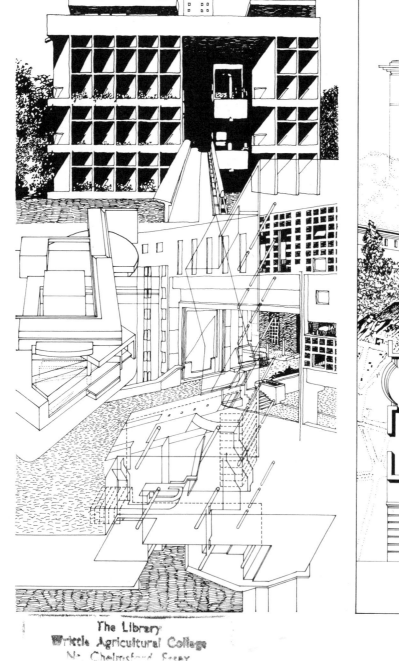

# Credits

# Index